Singing in a Strange Land

Praying and Acting with the Poor

William D. Lindsey, Ph.D.

Sheed & Ward

Sheed & Ward™ is a service of National Catholic Reporter
Publishing Company, Inc.

Library of Congress Catalog Card Number: 90-63488

ISBN: 1-55612-415-5

Published by: Sheed & Ward
                 115 E. Armour Blvd. P.O. Box 419492
                 Kansas City, MO 64141-6492

To order, call: (800) 333-7373

In a country ruled by the suppression of the truth, the imaginative writer is in a peculiar position of strength, for he or she can see through the lies without the need for evidence.
— A.N. Wilson, *Tolstoy*

Clearly, only those who anguish will sing new songs. Without anguish the new song is likely to be strident and just more royal fakery.
— Walter Brueggemann,
The Prophetic Imagination

In my utopia, human solidarity would be seen not as a fact to be recognized by clearing away "prejudice" or burrowing down to previously hidden depths but, rather, as a goal to be achieved. It is to be achieved not by inquiry but by imagination, the imaginative ability to see strange people as fellow sufferers. Solidarity is not discovered by reflection but created. It is created by increasing our sensitivity to the particular details of the pain and humiliation of the other, unfamiliar sorts of people. Such increased sensitivity makes it more difficult to marginalize people different from ourselves by thinking, "They do not feel it as *we* would," or "There must always be suffering, so why not let *them* suffer?"

This process of coming to see other human beings as "one of us" rather than as "them" is a matter of detailed description of what unfamiliar people are like and of redescription of what we ourselves are like. This is a task not for theory but for genres such ethnography, the journalist's report, the comic book, the docudrama, and, especially, the novel. . . . In my liberal utopia, this replacement [i.e., of the sermon by the novel as the principal vehicle of moral change] would receive a kind of recognition which it still lacks. That recognition would be part of a general turn against theory and toward narrative.
— Richard Rorty,
Contingency, Irony, and Solidarity

Contents

Acknowledgements

Scripture quotations are from the *Revised Standard Version Bible*, copyright 1946, 1956, 1971 by the Division of Christian Education of the National Council of the Churches of Christ in the USA and used by permission.

"Heal Me, My God" is reprinted from *Jewish Poets of Spain*, trans. by David Goldstein, with permission from David Higham Associates, London.

The prayers: "Let us remember tonight . . .," "Give us grace, O God . . .," are reprinted from *Prayers for Dark People*, by W.E.B. DuBois, ed. by Herbert Aptheker (Amherst: University of Massachusetts Press, 1980), copyright © 1980 by The University of Massachusetts Press.

Prayers from *The Prayers of African Religion*, by John S. Mbiti, *The Edge of Glory*, by David Adam, and *The Word Is The Seed* and *One Man's Prayers*, by George Appleton, are reprinted with permission of SPCK, London.

The extract Sura: 172-3 is taken from *The Koran Interpreted*, trans. A.J. Arberry, reproduced by kind permission of Unwin Hyman Ltd., (London: Allen & Unwin, 1955).

Prayers from *High Holiday Prayer Book*, compiled and edited by Rabbi Morris Silverman, Copyright © 1986, Bridgeport, CT, are reprinted by permission of Media Judaica, Inc., New York.

Passages from *A Testament of Hope*, by Martin Luther King, Jr., ed., James M. Washington (NY: Harper & Row, 1986) and Maurice Halbwachs, *The Collective Memory*, trans. Francis J. Ditter and Vida Yazdi Ditter and ed. Mary Douglas (NY: Harper & Row, 1980), reprinted with permission from Harper/Collins Publishers.

Prayers by Basil Naylor from Frank Colquhoun, *Contemporary Parish Prayers*, by Mary Craig from *Blessings*, by Martin Israel from *The Pain That Heals*, are all reproduced with kind permission of Hodder & Stoughton, Ltd., Dunton Green, Sevenoaks, Kent, England.

All prayers from *The Oxford Book of Prayer* are in common domain. The author wishes to acknowledge his indebtedness to the editors of this collection.

Preface

The scribe says that of making many books there is no end (Ecclesiastes 12:12). Not the least reason for this is that the list of those who have written a book—whether directly or indirectly—is endless. In this book I am indebted to more people than I can mention for constructive criticism, gentle nudgings in new directions, and that thankless yeoman's task, proofreading.

I want especially to thank Gregory Baum, Tad Dunne, June Fisher, SBS, Kathleen Gaffney, the late Stephen Goetz, OP, Roger Haight, SJ, Beatrice Jeffries, SBS, Clarence Menard, SM, Steve Schäfer, Rosemary Wesley, SCC, and Wolfram Weisse for reading the manuscript and making many helpful suggestions about it. Dorothee Sölle deserves a particular thank you for setting aside an afternoon in her busy schedule to talk with me about this book and the theme of solidarity with the poor: all this and *Abendbrot,* too. Many thanks are due as well to Bernard Lee, SM, for encouraging me to consider publication and for helping to bring the text to the attention of Sheed & Ward. Finally, I recall with fond memories the adult Sunday study class of the Corvallis, Oregon, Presbyterian church, who read and avidly discussed the book in its initial stages of composition; my undying gratitude goes particularly to Dick Clinton for "which-hunting" for me.

Two organizations provided invaluable assistance by funding time off for me to write the book and to travel to Hamburg to interview Dorothee Sölle. One of these was the Center for the Humanities of Oregon State University; the second was the Bush Foundation, through its faculty development grant to Xavier University.

Finally, I am painfully aware that I will always be in process as I learn to pray and act with the poor. That personal recognition began early in childhood, when my aunt, Katherine Simpson, urged me to *see* the state convicts who toiled in the hot sun to build Southern highways. What Aunt Kat began, Rosemary Wesley continued. To these two very dear mothers of my social conscience, I dedicate this book.

*   *   *

A note about certain emendations I have made to various texts reproduced in the *Biblical Reflections* and *Prayers from the Religions of the World* sections of the book. In prayers or other quoted passages, I have emended gender-exclusive texts by adding inclusive references in brackets.

Introduction

Praying and Acting with the Poor: Theological Considerations

---

*Christ made God manifest by making invisible people visible—
the poor, women, all those deprived of their rights.*
—Dorothee Sölle, *Of War and Love*

The Task of Christians Today: To Link Faith and Justice

The moment of history in which we live is one in which tremendous energies are being released within the Christian churches. An upwelling of creative energy is evident today in many aspects of Christian experience—in restructuring of ministries, for example, and in interreligious dialogue. But striking creativity is most notably apparent in two key areas, Christian spirituality and concern for social justice. In these two areas new movements and new theological reflection are transforming the face of the late twentieth-century churches.

Unfortunately, some contemporary believers play the new creative developments in spirituality and social justice concerns against each other. Many critics of the impulse for a new socially committed spirituality presuppose that a more engaged spiritual life has to ignore the demand for social transformation, or that a concern for justice constitutes an activism cut off from the spiritual life. My conviction—a deeply held one—is that the believer can and must build a bridge between the quest for a deeper spirituality and the struggle for justice. I have written this book out of that conviction.

My attempt to link spirituality and concern for justice is not unique. Some of the most promising theological reflection and creative developments within Christianity today are occurring within the theological movement called liberation theology. Liberation theology urges us to read the scriptures from the viewpoint of the poor, the marginal, the oppressed. Because this appeal is central to liberation theology, some Christians (particularly in the affluent sectors of the world) have concluded that liberation theology is merely a thin guise for a political activism that has little interest in the spiritual life.

In fact, nothing could be further from the truth. In the writings of liberation theologians, such as Gustavo Gutiérrez or Helder Câmara, one finds a strong insistence that a spirituality of solidarity with the poor must inform action for justice. Conversely, liberation theologians stress that an authentic spiritual life must connect itself to the quest for justice. In liberation theology spirituality and concern for social justice are inherently and necessarily linked; to say that one can exist without the other is to depart from what the Judaeo-Christian scriptures say, to distort their fundamental message. Liberation theologians are exploring the connections between spirituality and social justice, and are producing important work in the field of spirituality—they are articulating a Christian spirituality profoundly engaged in the struggle for justice.

A New Spirituality for North American Christians

I intend this book as a modest contribution to the contemporary theological enterprise of linking faith and justice. I am writing within and for a North American context. To be specific: I am writing for those North American Christians (such as I) who live in middle-class security and affluence and who seek to pray and act with the marginal of our society and the global community. Unfortunately, our security and affluence often cut us off from any effective contact with the poor, or any significant understanding of what it means to live on the margins of the social and economic power-structures of the world. Yet theologians and pastoral leaders in the Christian churches today are calling middle-class Christians to make the option for the poor.

I have confessional allegiance to the Roman Catholic church. The magisterium of that church encourages contemporary Catholics to pray and think with the poor, to link faith and justice. Papal documents, such as Pope Paul VI's *Evangelii Nuntiandi*, and pastoral letters, such as the recent U.S. bishops' letter *Economic Justice for All*, maintain that *all believers* are called to make the option for the poor, and that action for justice is a constitutive dimension of proclaiming the gospel. In the words of *Evangelii Nuntiandi*.

> The proclamation [of the gospel] must take place above all by witness, . . . a witness which requires presence, a sharing of life, and solidarity; in the carrying out of evangelisation this witness is an essential part, and often the first one (EN, 21-2).

Among other things, this means that we must challenge ourselves to see social structures from the vantage point of those who are excluded from participation in them—structures that deeply affect the lives of the marginated and make the realization of their full human potential difficult.

One of the roadblocks that middle-class Christians encounter as they seek to look at social structures through the eyes of the poor is that they have *little imagination* about what it means—concretely, experientially—to be *poor*. I have lectured in schools and churches in the United States and Canada, and I have learned that across the continent, the North American churches are crippled by a poverty of the imagination as they work to understand the situation of the poor. Biblical scholar Walter Brueggemann thinks that we first-world Christians live within a culture that *deliberately* suppresses imagination. Brueggemann argues that imagination always represents a threat to the status quo, because the exercise of imagination permits us to see through the self-justifying rationales of the powerful and envisage alternative ways of organizing society. Thus cultures that do not want radical social change restrict imagination, perhaps (as in our consumer culture) simply by pretending that it is simply impossible to imagine anything other than the vapid iconography of Madison Avenue or Hollywood. As Brueggemann insists, "Our culture is competent to implement almost anything and to imagine almost nothing."[1]

Our churches urge us to give faces to the poor, to see the poor as persons and not a faceless mass or a lifeless category of sociological textbooks (see *Economic Justice for All*, 172-4). To do this, we must attempt to project our imaginations into the situations of the poor. This book endeavors to help North American Christians make the leap of imagination that is necessary if we are to pray and act with the poor.

To achieve solidarity with the poor requires a new spirituality. And a new spirituality of praying with the poor demands the transformation of our imaginations about what it means to be poor. In learning to pray with the poor, we are learning to pray with the victims of society, with those whose voices are so suppressed that they seldom reach the ears of the privileged. A spirituality of praying with the poor should make us North American Christians uncomfortably aware that *we* are the privileged—and that we cannot be faithful disciples of Jesus if we are complacent about being so. Praying with the poor engenders in us a spiritual restlessness that may call us to make drastic changes in how we view the world, in how we use the resources available to us, in how we choose lifestyles.

The Social Construction of the Human Person

In addition to the curtailment of imagination, our society places another obstacle in the way of those who wish to pray with the poor. This is the atomistic individualism that pervades our culture. We commonly think of the person as a self-contained unit who exists over against and in isolation from the social order. We imagine that one becomes a person by claiming an individuality that stands apart from society. Our literature is saturated with images of the solitary individual who struggles to be authentic to himself or herself against all odds. Our media and films foster the

---

1.   Walter Brueggemann, *The Prophetic Imagination* (Philadelphia: Fortress, 1978), 45.

notion that one can truly be a self-made man or woman—all one has to do is work hard enough.

Because we accept these myths uncritically, we lack imagination for perceiving how social structures impact on—indeed, even create—persons. A key insight of modern sociological analysis is that *human persons are socially constituted*. This insight is capable of being misunderstood in a reductionistic sense that implies that persons are *merely* the product of economic or political forces. But properly understood, it points to an important truth about the human person, one often overlooked in our culture. This truth is that we do not make ourselves: we achieve our personhood only within a cultural matrix that shapes us from the moment we are born. For example, *language* determines us as persons. If we wish to communicate, we must have recourse to that set of socially determined verbal symbols we call language. Language is by nature social: its meaning preexists us, is defined apart from us. By using it, we partake of socially constituted symbols, symbols that in turn constitute us. Even when we express our "private" thoughts to others, we do so by means of words that stand between us and the other.

We are socially constituted by history as well. As William Faulkner constantly observed, the past is not really past, it is not even over yet. Faulkner's brilliant novels meditate on how a stream of occurrences that began in the past still affects the present. Or, to adopt another metaphor, from the moment of our birth we all carry our history on our shoulders. Our culture's belief that we are all born with equal chances to find economic fulfillment and social betterment is fatuous; this belief does not withstand critical scrutiny. Many of us are so handicapped from the moment of birth by the vicious history of poverty into which we are born, that we can move out of that history only with pain and struggle. *Are* most black Americans, who even today bear the burden of the history of enslavement, or most Appalachian whites, who bear the burden of historic economic exploitation, *really* born as free and equal as most middle-class Americans?

Another social structure that constructs us as persons is the community of memory into which we are born. As sociologist Maurice Halbwachs points out, we remember as individuals only from within a community of memory. The tradition of our family,

nation, church, or local community orients our attention to particular past events: we remember *this* and not *that*, and we interpret
the memory in this way and not that way. As Halbwachs notes,
"A person remembers only by situating himself within the viewpoint of one or several groups and one or several currents of collective thought."[2]

This insight has enormous implications for what the Christian
churches call *tradition*. It implies that in our faith journey we never
believe as single individuals, but from within the tradition that our
faith community hands on to us. And it also implies that the
church has a primary role to play in shaping our faith by handing
tradition on in a way that continuously confronts us with the *living
and unsettling memory* of Jesus and those who have witnessed to
him over the centuries. The Christian church is fundamentally a
community of *memoria Christi*: the church exists primarily to remember Jesus through listening to the gospels and celebrating the
eucharist, an act that represents (re-presents) the Lord to us—liter-
ally so, since the memorial meal re-calls in a way that makes present what is recalled. As theologian Johannes Baptist Metz argues,
this memory of Jesus handed on in the church's tradition is not a
priceless antique but a *dangerous* memory, one that has the potential to deconstruct all the compromises that Christians make
throughout history with the powers that be in the world.

In the broadest possible sense, society makes us by providing a
socio-economic and cultural matrix within which we achieve our
unique personhood. An important conclusion follows from this.
That is, since the social and economic systems that construct the
person are shaped by human beings and are not the product of
nature or the result of divine revelation, they are subject to change.
If the structures of a society (for example, its economic structures)
thwart the ability of many in that society to achieve full personhood, then one cannot change the situation of *individuals* without
addressing and changing the *structures* within which individuals
live.

---

2.   Maurice Halbwacks, *The Collective Memory*, trans. Francis J. Ditter and Vida
Yazdi Ditler, ed. Mary Douglas (New York: Harper & Row, 1980), 33.

We need to allow this insight to contribute new depth to our understanding of what it means to pray with the poor. We can pray in union with the poor only when we seek to understand and identify the ways in which the poor are constituted by society as marginal and voiceless persons. Christian spirituality, then, is by its very nature social and political. Spirituality of course concerns itself with personal union with God. But since one cannot speak of the person apart from social structures—because these structures constitute the person—then concern for personal union with God must simultaneously be a concern to fathom social systems and to work to make them enable all persons to achieve their full human potential.

North American Christianity has difficulty understanding spirituality in this way because the atomistic individualism of North American culture blinds many North American Christians to the social dimensions of the spiritual life. On the premise that the individual is autonomous, we have elaborated a spirituality that privatizes the spiritual life. We think of the spiritual life as an inward journey—and our imagination sees the person's journey within as *occurring away from* society. On this basis, we have constructed religious systems that sharply distinguish between *this world* (the "secular" world of politics and economics) and *that world* (the "religious" world of prayer and worship). This division of labor even leads us to regard action for peace, better jobs, or adequate medical care as "political" rather than religious.

All Authentic Christian Spirituality Is Social

I am increasingly convinced that there is no such thing as the solitary individual, or the solitary individual's inward quest. Since this bald statement can easily be misunderstood, let me explain what I mean. If the spiritual life is in any sense an inward quest, it is so because we turn inward to encounter deep within ourselves that which transcends our finite selves. In theological terms, we find our deepest and true selves in prayer, but we do so by discovering God as the ground of our being, God who is other than the self—indeed, to use the classic phrase of Rudolf Otto, the Other who is *mysterium tremendum et fascinans*. At the still point of the self we find meaning that, like language itself, preexists and stands outside us. The inward journey is a dead end if it ceases with the self alone, with the sense that the boundaries of the self have been confirmed and made more rigid. Authentic prayer, it seems to me, makes us more aware of how deeply we are connected to God and to all other human beings.

Several modern thinkers offer fascinating insights into the links between the inner journey of imagination and the outward world of social reality. In his investigations of dreams, C.G. Jung suggested that the psyche of the individual enfolds archetypal symbols, symbols he thought to be common to all persons. If Jung was correct, then a journey that appears to be prototypically private—the inward journey of the dream—is not private and individual at all. Like the inward journey of prayer, it issues in shared meaning. In Jungian analysis we achieve personal integration by learning to decipher and hear the archetypal symbols that speak to us in the depths of our psyches. When we think ourselves to be going most deeply within, we are moving toward a place in which our "private" thought joins to the symbolic substratum underlying the "private" thought of all other humans. Jung theorized that human thought originates in the subconscious, the place in which archetypal meaning resides. In his view, the subconscious of the individual connects to the collective unconscious of the race. This implies that we are able to communicate at all because there is commonality in the deep structures of our minds, and in the chthonic archetypes that inform those deep structures.

Another thinker who links the imaginative inner life of the individual to social reality is philosopher Ernst Bloch. In his masterwork *The Principle of Hope*, Bloch argues that the human community has given surprisingly little systematic thought to the future. He maintains that we *can* think about the future, in the first place by paying attention to the ways in which we imagine the future in daydreams. In Bloch's view, such imaginative dreaming is not idle utopianism, but an attempt to project ourselves individually and as a human community into the *real* future, the future that *really* exists as the absolute goal of history. Our daydreams recognize that the present can take another shape that more adequately realizes its potential. In Bloch's view, our ability to imagine the world differently in daydreams implies that we recognize a standard by which the present can be judged adequate or inadequate: this standard is the goal of history, or to use Christian theological language, the reign of God.

Such an interpretation of imaginative dreaming clearly conjoins the individual and the social. If Bloch is correct, even our "private" dreams of the future meld with those social dreams in which the human community projects itself forward toward the goal of history. Our "private" probing of the trajectory of history in fantasy links us to the shared quest of all human beings for a better and fuller life. Thus Bloch insists that we ought to pay much more attention to our attempts to imagine the future, because it is in dreaming together that we see how the future can be and how we can begin to move toward it.

Thinkers such as Jung and Bloch have opened important new doors for Christian theology in the twentieth century. Theologians today are exploring the connections between the "private" spiritual quest and the quest for a more humane world. As these theologians note, the scriptures explode our neat demarcations between the person (as closed inner world) and society, between sacred and secular. The Jewish prophets shout that Yahweh yearns for social justice. Yahweh wants better jobs, adequate medical care and housing for human beings: to work for these, the prophets insist, is not to do secular work, but the will of God. The prophets proclaim that one cannot worship God in a hermetically sealed sacred space while ignoring God's demand for justice—as though to enter church or temple is to leave the world behind. No: true worship is to do justice; to ritualize our relationship with God while violating the justice demands of the covenant is to void worship of all significance. Jesus stands in this prophetic tradition. Much of his salvific work is, by the canons of today, secular. He heals, he calls for release of prisoners and subversion/transformation of social structures so that the last shall be first and the first last.

When we accept the call of theologians today to read the scriptures in light of the recognition that persons are socially constructed, we move toward a new spirituality of praying with the poor. This spirituality takes as one of its fundamental starting-points the awareness that we *cannot* pray in isolation from the poor. We cannot do so in the first place because this isolation is a fiction; as persons we are intimately linked to all other persons in the social network. As a character in one of Wendell Berry's stories puts the point, "The way we are, we are members of each other. All of us. Everything. The difference ain't in who is a member and who is not, but in who knows it and who don't."[3] One of the glaring failures of North American individualism is its refusal to acknowledge the manifold interconnections between persons and classes in our society. The middle class *needs* those who are economically exploited; it does so above all in order to maintain its affluence. How *we* live and how *they* live are interconnected. To pray as if these connections do not exist, or as if we owe only charity and not justice to the poor among us, is to participate in our culture's willful blindness regarding the social network in which we all live.

Furthermore, we cannot pray in isolation from the poor and be faithful to the preaching of the prophets or of Jesus. If we wish to root our faith in this biblical tradition, we must learn to pray with the poor. I am writing this book to describe a way—not *the* way, but *a* way—for us to learn to pray with the poor. The way I sketch is that of using our imaginations to probe the connections between our world and theirs, to enter the world in which the poor live today. Such imaginative prayer ought to enliven our imagination about ways to restructure our societies so that all of us have the opportunity to live fuller human existences. Praying and acting for justice are two sides of a coin. There needs to be a constant circulation between our prayer and action, so that one feeds into and deepens the other.

The Poor Are the Marginal

It is time that I clarify what I mean when I speak of praying with the poor. When I use this phrase, I do not mean that we understand what impoverished people endure simply because we read about them or have sympathy for them. Such sentimental "praying" with the poor actually divorces us from real connection to the poor. It alienates us from the poor by demeaning them and in the end reinforcing our own sense of superiority. It has little to

---

3.   Wendell Berry, *The Wild Birds* (San Francisco: North Point, 1986), 136-7.

do with actual knowledge of the poor as persons. In fact, such sentimentalized prayer with the poor presupposes a patronizing idea of charity—that is, that we actually owe nothing to the poor, and that what we give, we give out of our generosity and largesse. As theologian Dorothee Sölle asks, "What do we really mean when we use that grand word 'solidarity'? How do we leave the noun behind and find the right verb?"[4] To pray and act with the poor is an arduous activity, one in which we leave behind our easy answers and enter a process in which the poor become our teachers.

We need to develop the imagination to enter the situation of the poor and to pray from within this situation precisely so that we can *stop stereotyping* and romanticizing the poor. Concretely, this means that our prayer with the poor is not alive unless it issues in action to effect justice for the poor. Our prayer stops being sentimental and moves toward actual knowledge of the poor when it opens us to the possibility of acting with the poor to reshape the structures of society so that all of us, and particularly the downtrodden and the outcast, can have more humane existences. Conversely, this action for justice deepens and enriches our prayer. It teaches us to pray more honestly in solidarity with the poor.

We need as well to clarify the meaning of the term "poor." The word not uncommonly connotes a collective entity, a sterile category of social classification; careless and unreflective use of the term can thus contribute to demeaning and stereotyping of the poor. Perhaps we can flesh out the term by stretching our imagination about what being poor entails. We can do so by imagining poor people as *disempowered* people, people whose experience is that of being a counter in a game over which they have little control. As the American Catholic bishops argue in their pastoral letter, *Economic Justice for All*, to be poor is at base to experience *marginalization*: the poor are those who are pushed to the margins of society and have little chance of participating at any effective level in the social and economic structuring of that society. Clearly, the term "poor" thus denotes the actual poor, the physi-

---

4. Dorothee Sölle, *Of War & Love*, trans. Rita and Robert Kimber (Maryknoll, NY: Orbis, 1983), 133.

cally poor, the shocking percentage of the global community who exist close to starvation. But the term also refers to those who are outcast and disempowered in other ways.

The marginal include those who are excluded for racial or sexual reasons, the elderly, and other social groups. Perhaps we should shy away from the attempt to expand the term "poor" in the gospels to include those who have wealth and power, but who seek "inner" poverty. It is a typical maneuver of North American Christians in face of the hard sayings of Jesus about the need for his disciples to be poor. But this semantic maneuver is a verbal camouflage to protect us from the shocking impact of Jesus' sayings. But we should perhaps also beware of a reductionism that equates poverty with material poverty. As Donal Dorr notes,

> These [the poor as the marginal] would include those who are economically poor, the groups that are politically marginalised or oppressed, people discriminated against on sexual grounds, peoples that have been culturally silenced or oppressed, and those who have been religiously disinherited or deprived.[5]

I hope that readers of this book will keep such nuances in mind when they read the term "poor."

As we seek to stretch our imagination about the poor, it may be helpful to imagine society as a series of concentric circles emanating from a small, inner circle of power. The poor are those who exist at the edges around the outermost circle. They have been pushed to the margins, outside the circles of power. Those who occupy the small inner circle of power (on a global level, they are almost exclusively first-world white males) maintain their power by creating and manipulating the symbols around which a given society revolves. Think of the power that the advertising industry (itself an adjunct of the powerful commercial sector) exercises over our lives by defining the symbols of normalcy, the symbols to which we "ought" to aspire. Think of the power of this industry's symbols of the beautiful. Note how these symbols implicitly mar-

---

5.   Donal Dorr, *Option for the Poor: A Hundred Years of Vatican Social Teaching,* (Maryknoll, NY: Orbis, 1983), 4.

ginate groups of people, either by ignoring them or by suggesting that they are less than normal or beautiful.

The poor in a given society are systematically marginated, distorted, and suppressed by the controlling symbols of a society. Note the word *suppressed*: one of the most powerful functions of the inner circle of a given society is to suppress alternative systems of symbols, alternative imaginations about how the society might be organized. The example of beauty is apt. We reflect too seldom about how our definitions of the beautiful presuppose a cultural consensus, a cultural decision to call this beautiful and that ugly. It is not an accident that the symbols of beauty emanating from the power centers of a society hold up the powerful themselves as the beautiful. Flip through the pages of any mainstream magazine in the United States, and note *who* are the models put forth for our emulation. Then think about how these symbols simultaneously project a model of the beautiful and strongly suppress alternative models. As Thomas Cullinan notes,

> The main text of our culture, involved so closely as it is with economic processes, is written by and for those already in the main text, and because of the processes at work, those in the margin are kept there. . . . The main text not only produces the margins as part of its being written, but needs the margins for its very existence.[6]

The symbols of the center both present themselves as the final word about beauty or normalcy, and define other symbols as less than beautiful or normal.

Imaginative Prayer, Imaginative Action

The preceding reflections provide greater depth and texture for two of the key concepts of the method of prayer set forth in *Singing in a Strange Land*. Another key term also demands close attention. This is the term *imagination*. What does it mean to pray by

---

6.   Thomas Cullinan, *If the Eye Be Sound*, (Slough, Eng.: St. Paul, 1975), 75-7.

projecting one's imagination into the situation of a poor person, or to act on the basis of a new imagination about the social order that creates this situation? Part of the answer to these questions lies in the Christian tradition. *Singing in a Strange Land*'s appeal to imagination is not unprecedented: use of the imagination in meditative prayer is a venerable and ancient practice in many schools of Christian spirituality. In the Roman Catholic tradition, for example, several masters of the spiritual life, including Ignatius of Loyola, Teresa of Avila, and Julian of Norwich, have sketched brilliant methods for applying imagination as one meditates. Ignatius and Teresa teach us to place ourselves imaginatively within scenes in the life of Christ. Julian instructs us to use our imaginations to delve into the mysteries of the divine nature—for example, by imagining the world as a grain of sand cuddled lovingly in the hand of the Divine Mother. In the Protestant tradition, George Fox and John Bunyan similarly employ imagination as a tool of spiritual understanding. In calling for the use of imagination to pray with the poor, *Singing in a Strange Land* mines a rich vein of Christian spirituality.

Though the tradition has been somewhat slower to link imaginative prayer and imaginative concern for social change, classical spiritual works nonetheless contain some important hints about how one might use imagination to pray and act with the poor. One seldom thinks of the nineteenth-century cloistered Carmelite Thérèse of Lisieux as a champion of social justice. After all, the conventional interpretation has it, she spent her short life within the walls of a cloister, and her knowledge of the world around her was extremely limited. But Thérèse's autobiography, *Story of A Soul*, suggests that such an interpretation may not be entirely accurate. Throughout her autobiography, Thérèse expresses a concern to fathom the workings of the society in which she lived—indeed, even to affect the course of that society and move it in the direction of social justice through her solitary prayer.

A passage describing her solicitude for Pranzini, a murderer condemned to death in 1887, indicates the tenor of her thought. Though the passage refers to the time before Thérèse entered Carmel, it captures insights about linking imaginative prayer to social concerns that were to form the framework of her spirituality after she made her religious profession. In the passage, Thérèse describes how she sought to project herself into the situation of Pranzini as he faced execution and to pray imaginatively from within that situation. When Thérèse read in the newspapers that Pranzini had kissed a crucifix offered to him as he mounted the scaffold, she became convinced that her prayer had been effective.[7]

Thérèse's account of the "conversion" of Pranzini admittedly employs the sentimental terms of nineteenth-century French piety. Yet it contains a heart of steel. What is remarkable in the passage is that there is no suspicion of condemnation of Pranzini, no sense that he was a lost sinner who deserved his lot. Rather, there is a strong suggestion that Pranzini (and other condemned criminals) deserves compassion and hope. In an account of prototypically "inward-journey" spirituality, one discovers an opening to a spirituality that links faith and action for justice—the seeds of a faith-inspired awareness that society may share in the guilt of those it judges criminals, since society allows the conditions that breed crime to exist.

The method of imaginative prayer set forth in *Singing in a Strange Land* roots itself in the Christian tradition in another important way. Many of the most ancient Christian spiritual writers, the desert fathers and mothers of early monasticism, speak of the need for a prayer that moves from the head to the heart. One of the primary tasks of the spiritual life is to unite the two, to make the head and heart pray together. In recent centuries Western Christian spirituality has been overly rational. It has been a spirituality of mental "exercises" in which one reads and meditates on what one has read, or in which one listens to a sermon or lecture and then prays in light of what one has heard. What is lacking in such spirituality is appeal to the intuitive and affective dimensions of the person. As persons we live out of the heart. Prayer that develops the imagination unites the head and the heart. One of the primary virtues of such prayer is that it links the heart with the head in a way that enables the heart to inform the head, and the head to reach the heart. When I speak of using imagination in the chapters that follow, I have in mind a type of prayer in which both

---

7. *Story of a Soul*, trans. John Clarke (Washington, DC: ICS, 1975), 99-101.

head and heart strive to comprehend the situation of poor persons, and to generate a new imagination about how society can be arranged so that no one among us need be poor.

In conclusion, to pray with the poor is to learn a new language. To do so, we must listen to the poor, and must begin to speak haltingly from what we learn by this listening. This task of learning to speak the language of the poor is a lifelong task. If we begin to learn this language, then we shall also begin to sing the strange song of praise that arises from the strange land of the poor to God their maker and liberator, our maker and liberator.

Guide to Using *Singing in a Strange Land*

The body of the text of *Singing in a Strange Land* contains seven imaginative journeys, accompanied by scriptural reflections, prayers from world religions, and actions on behalf of justice. Each imaginative journey focuses on a particular poor person (or persons) in North America today. The exception to this rule is the third journey, which deals with a Latin American *campesino*. I include this journey to indicate how decisively North American political and economic structures impact third-world workers.

My reason for giving primary attention to the poor among us, rather than in the global community, is simple. It seems to me that we need first and foremost to learn to see the poor who are in our midst. One of the more destructive American myths is the belief that poverty is earned, and that poverty exists in North America only when people choose to be poor. The flip side of the myth is equally destructive: this is the belief that America is the land of opportunity in which poverty has been vanquished, that we have no really poor people among us. Both tangents of thought disguise or discount poverty in the United States.

Of course we need to expand our vision to a global level as well. For this reason, I have included in the *Actions* section of each exercise an analysis of American poverty that links it to global economic and political issues or structures. One final remark about the selection process underlying the imaginative journeys. The list of the poor in *Singing in a Strange Land* is by no means exhaustive. The catalog of marginal people that follows is not a complete index of all the marginal in our society and world today. The stories the characters tell are *representative* stories. One of the primary tasks of those who seek to pray and act with the poor is to analyze their own particular social situation. Who are the poor among us, in this town or parish or diocese? The answers to that question will vary greatly from place to place.

Imaginative Journeys

Each section begins with an imaginative journey. These are all first-person narratives. The journeys (and the biblical reflections, prayers, and actions that follow) can be used either in private meditation or public worship. In either case, I suggest that the journeys be read and pondered as the classic works on spirituality indicate that one ought to read and ponder any meditative passage. That is, the setting ought to be one conducive to meditation: quiet, peaceful, unharried. In such a setting, the imaginative journeys can be read slowly and meditatively. Readers (or listeners, if the journey is incorporated into a worship service) should attempt to savor the journey and to open themselves to the presence of God and to more profound understanding of the situation of the poor.

Each imaginative journey is constructed to end with a line intended to draw the the reader/listener into a moment of meditative silence. The concluding lines of each journey reinforce the connections between the reader/listener and the person speaking in the journey. They also suggest the manifold effects of our shared social reality upon the person whose journey is presented. An analogy with haiku poetry is not inexact (though the journeys are far more verbose than haiku!). Haiku ends pointing beyond itself, to open the subject of the poem to further silent reflection—as if the poem self-destructs and demonstrates to the reader that silence is, after all, the better way for one to approach that to which the poem points. I have read one of the imaginative journeys in public worship, and I found that reading slowly, quietly, and ending with a moment of silence was a very effective method of presenting the journey.

My hope is that each imaginative journey will lead the reader/listener to pray with the poor, and to begin to think of significant ways in which he or she, and we as church and human community, can alter the structures that allow so much poverty in our midst. Each imaginative journey seeks to awaken the reader to the many ways in which the society in which we live constitues some of us as marginal, and so to our responsibility to and for those made marginal by our society.

Scriptural Meditations and Prayers from the Religions of the World

A series of scriptural reflections and prayers from the religions of the world follows each imaginative journey. These resources constitute an invitation for individual readers or worship groups to pray more effectively with the poor. The scriptural meditations include passages from the Jewish and Christian scriptures and brief prayerful reflections on these passages. The prayers from world religions include prayers from various religious traditions, and poems or other literary selections by various writers.

As with the imaginative journeys, these resources can be used in different ways. Individual readers may find that the scriptural meditations and prayers provide an entry point for further study of the Judaeo-Christian scriptures or the religious traditions of the world and the wealth they contain for those who seek to pray and act with the poor. Or a particular prayer or scripture passage may cast new light on how a reader can pray with the poor. Those who wish to employ these resources in public worship can choose prayers or scriptural meditations that are most useful for their particular community of worship. Several of the prayers included in each exercise are rather didactic. Didactic prayer is perhaps more suited to public worship than to private prayer. While it may irritate or alienate the person praying alone, it often proves to be an effective tool of public worship; it sweeps the congregation up as it pounds on a central point or theme of the worship of a given service.

The selection of scriptures or prayers that appears in each exercise is no more exhaustive or definitive than is the list of marginal persons whose stories are told in the book. Readers should treat the selection as a starting-point for further investigation; they should examine their own religious traditions and other traditions to find further resources for praying and acting with the poor. One of the recognitions I hope to awaken in readers is that all of the religious traditions of the world contain vast unexplored resources for praying with the poor. The Judeo-Christian scriptures have so much to say about the poor in our midst today that I have found it very difficult to limit the passages I wished to include.

Actions on Behalf of Justice for the Poor

At the conclusion of each section is a list of possible actions on behalf of justice for those whose voice is represented by the imaginative journey of that section. With each action, I provide suggestions about how readers may initiate the action. The explanatory information accompanying each action is also intended to sketch in more detail the social background of the marginalization depicted in each imaginative journey.

Many of the activities listed envisage concerted action or study by a parish or church group. In churches or parishes where such groups do not exist, it will be necessary to organize them. Those doing so will find very helpful information about organizing a parish educational program in *Building Economic Justice*; a reference to this resource appears in the annotated bibliography below.

The actions listed are by no means *all* the possible actions on behalf of justice for the poor people whose stories appear in *Singing in a Strange Land*. How one acts for justice will depend very much on one's particular situation, on the needs of one's own community. Most readers will be able to think of acts other than those listed that are more suited to their circumstances, and more likely to be effective. And as with the actions themselves, so with the suggestions about how to initiate them: these suggestions must be tailored to the unique situation of the group or person doing the action. The point is for readers and groups to liberate their imaginations, to open the imagination to the multitude of ways in which we *can* act to change the structures of society and not merely to offer charity to the poor. The point is also that we can never be done acting. There is always more to do.

Finally, as an aid for study, I have included a brief annotated bibliography of resources for the entire set of exercises, and a brief bibliography of resources for each exercise. Each set of actions contains suggestions for study; when these suggestions refer readers to a specific book or other study guide, the reference is to a resource listed in the bibliography at the end of that set of actions.

Resources for Further Study

Credence Cassettes, 115 Armour Blvd., P.O. Box 419491, Kansas City, MO 64141-6491. A source for audio and visual resources dealing with various social justice issues of concern to the churches today.

Dorr, Donal. *Option for the Poor: A Hundred Years of Vatican Social Teaching.* Maryknoll, NY: Orbis, 1983. A concise and readable presentation of papal teaching from *Rerum Novarum* to the present, with emphasis on the option for the poor.

Fagan, Harry. *Empowerment: Skills for Parish Social Action.* NY: Paulist, 1979. A useful guide for ways to create and implement social action programs at the parish level. Discusses how parishes can strategize to deal with social issues in their particular area.

Gremillion, Joseph, ed. *The Gospel of Justice and Peace: Catholic Social Teaching Since Pope John.* Maryknoll, NY: Orbis, 1976. An indispensable resource for those interested in the Catholic tradition. Contains the basic social documents of the Catholic magisterium from the period of Popes John XXIII and Paul VI.

Haughey, John, ed. *The Faith That Does Justice.* NY: Paulist, 1977. Essays dealing with the theological foundations for a spirituality of praying and acting with the poor.

Holland, Joe and Peter Henriot. *Social Analysis: Linking Faith and Justice.* Rev. ed. Maryknoll, NY: Orbis, 1980. An excellent introduction both to the theological foundation of a spirituality that links faith and justice, and to practical ways to engage in social analysis.

Kavanaugh, John. *Following Christ in a Consumer Society.* Maryknoll, NY: Orbis, 1981. A meditation on the implications of living the gospel in contemporary American society. Invaluable as a tool for provoking thought and discussion about what radical discipleship means in the cultural setting in which Americans find themselves today.

National Conference of Catholic Bishops. *Economic Justice for All.* Washington, DC: U.S. Catholic Conference, 1986. A pastoral letter in which the American Catholic bishops call on American Catholics to inform their consciences about the implications of the gospel for economic life, about the poor in American society today, and about options for acting to create a more just society. An invaluable study guide for the pastoral is *Building Economic Justice* (Washington, DC: U.S. Catholic Conference, 1987).

Neal, Marie Augusta. *A Socio-Theology of Letting Go*. NY: Paulist, 1977. Seminal reflections on a new spirituality linking faith and justice—including acknowledging the links between first-world greed and third-world poverty, and attempting to respond by creating a new lifestyle for first-world Christians.

The Other Side. The Other Side, 300 W. Apsley St., Philadelphia, PA 19144. A journal focusing on action for justice rooted in discipleship.   Although not exclusively Catholic in orientation, frequently includes articles by leaders of Catholic social justice action, such as Daniel Berrigan.

Santa Ana, Julio de. *Good News to the Poor*. Geneva: World Council of Churches, 1977. A theological examination of the church's role vis-a-vis the poor, by the director of the Department of Development of the World Council of Churches.

Sojourners. Sojourners Magazine, Box 29272, Washington, DC 20078-5290. A journal exploring the radical implications of Christian discipleship.   Draws primarily, though not exclusively, on evangelical Christian traditions.

Wallis, Jim. *The Call to Conversion*. San Francisco: Harper & Row, 1982. A thorough and moving discussion of what conversion entails (socially, politically) in the world in which we now live. Written from an evangelical Christian standpoint by the editor of *Sojourners*.

Wogaman, J. Philip. *Economics and Ethics*. Philadelphia: Fortress, 1986. Very helpful and readable Christian ethical evaluation of various economic systems, with suggestions about how alternative systems might be organized.

Chapter One

Jim, A Homeless Man

The Imaginative Journey

You and I . . . we are not so different from one another.

I had a good upbringing. I expected a bright future. When I finished college, I opened an accounting agency and married my high school sweetheart, Edy. We bought a new house in the suburbs and began to plan for a family. When James, Jr., came along, the agency was doing well and we decided to have a second child.

It was after Francine was born that things began to fall apart. Edy and I felt that we were doing everything right, but everthing started to go wrong at once. With two children and more and more bills, I felt I needed to work as hard as I could. I told myself that I had to provide a good living for my family, a bright future for James and Francine. I fell into a pattern of working around the clock.

I have to admit that I've never handled stress well. The more I felt everything depended on me, the harder I worked. The harder I worked, the more inadequate I felt. I started to develop ulcers. I couldn't sleep at night. I felt hollowed out inside.

One morning as I left for the office, I didn't see Francine on her tricycle in the driveway. I backed over her. She lived several hours after we rushed her to the hospital. As Edy and I sat beside her, she whimpered and called for us. Even now, I wake up at night in a cold sweat feeling that I'm trying to reach through a glass wall as Francine is dying: I can see her, but I can't touch her and make her know she's not alone.

Though Edy knew what I had done was not deliberate, it was clear to me that she held deep anger against me. This made me question myself even more, castigate myself more relentlessly: if only you had looked into the driveway; if only you had checked the rearview mirror. The more I began to tell myself these things, the more Edy's silence seemed to spread, until a pool of silence lay between us.

I started to wonder if I had killed my daughter because I cared more for my work than my family.

I began to drink and neglect the agency. Bills mounted. Edy and I started to argue. When I came home late and drunk, she would meet me at the door in stony silence. We often lay in bed with our backs to one another, each thinking, never speaking. James, Jr., suffered. He had been a model student. His grades slipped, and teachers sent home notes saying that he was exhibiting problem behavior in class.

One day I snapped. It all seemed too much. I got into the car and drove aimlessly. As I went faster and faster, I came to a bridge and thought that it would be easy to end our suffering by running the car into the railing. My family would collect the insurance, I would be out of the way, all would be well. I resisted, but something had died inside. From that day, I stopped going to work. After I had lain in bed for several weeks and the agency had entered into financial crisis, Edy insisted that I see a psychiatrist.

The doctor diagnosed me as severely depressed and encouraged me to spend some time in a mental health ward of a hospital. I checked into the hospital. The day that I entered the hospital was the last day I ever saw Edy and James, Jr. They didn't visit me, and when I called home I found that the number had been disconnected. After a week, Edy wrote a letter asking if she could sell the house. I didn't know what to do; I signed the papers to give her permission. Edy made the sale and moved to her mother's retirement home across the country. I felt like dying. My depression deepened, and the doctor tried more and more medication. After a month and a half, I felt that the drugs were doing nothing for me. Against the doctor's advice, I left the hospital.

With no house to go to and bills I couldn't pay, the only answer seemed to be to live on the street. At first I had no idea of how to do that. Gradually I learned.

Yesterday and today were typical days on the street for me. The shelter on 7th Street only takes people who haven't stayed there in the past month. The other shelter, on Van Buren Boulevard, will not take anyone who has been drinking. I had been to 7th Street on the past weekend, and I got enough money yesterday to buy some cheap wine, so Van Buren would not take me.

I spent the night in the doorway of McMath's insurance firm. It was cold. My coat is several sizes too large; I got it at one of the shelters. I use it to cover with on cold nights. My buddy George slept next to me. The shared warmth makes it possible to doze off several times between dark and daylight. We drank together from our bottles. George had several packages of salted nuts. That was our dinner. Neither of us has bathed in several days, but we have long since learned not to care about things like that.

As we dozed people walked past and didn't see us. A group of teenagers coming from the Majestic Theater decided to have fun by poking at us and laughing. When we lay in silence, they went on. The most difficult nights are when someone decides to use force to move us on. That someone is often a cop.

This morning was clear and crisp. I awoke with stale vomit in my beard and on the side of my face. When George and I were both awake, we decided to walk to the riverbank where street folk often gather to make fires to warm themselves and talk. Sometimes someone has some coffee. We brew it in tin cans and share it around the group. We were in luck today. There was coffee and a bag of doughnuts that a passerby had left with Lucy.

After we had eaten breakfast, we went to line up for the soup at the First Methodist Church down on Main. This is always hot, but the taste varies. At one time I was finicky. I still have preferences, but I eat what I can get when I can get it.

When lunch was over George and I separated. I stood outside the Sears store and panhandled. Most people ignored me. Some verbally abused me. You might not believe it, but this is better than being ignored. A few folks gave me change. One offered me a religious tract: "Are you saved? God prospers those who trust him. Get right with God, and you'll have showers of blessings."

I collected $6.92. George got $3.28. When we pooled our money, we had enough to buy two bottles of cheap wine. That was dinner, that and several packs of cheese crackers George managed to pick up from a food cart when the vendor wasn't looking.

That was my yesterday. This was my today.

I am just like you . . . a human being.

Scriptural Reflections

The Word of God

In days to come the mountain of the Lord's house shall be established as the highest of mountains, and shall be raised up above the hills. Peoples shall stream to it, and many nations shall come and say: "Come, let us go up to the mountain of the Lord, to the house of the God of Jacob; that he may teach us his ways and that we may walk in his paths." For out of Zion shall go forth instruction, and the word of the Lord from Jerusalem. He shall judge between many peoples, and shall arbitrate between strong nations far away; they shall beat their swords into plowshares, and their spears into pruning hooks; nation shall not lift up sword against nation, neither shall they learn war any more; but they shall all sit under their own vines and under their own fig trees, and no one shall make them afraid; for the mouth of the Lord of hosts has spoken. (Micah 4:1-4).

Prayer Response

Lord, your prophets describe the fulfillment of your will for us as a time of plenty for all. You call us to work that your will be done on earth. You have given us the earth with its abundance so that all may eat and bless your name. Your will is that all sit under their own vine and fig trees.

Strengthen us to labor against those who seek to hoard the treasures of the earth, allowing a few to be overfed while many starve, a few to be housed in exorbitant luxury while many lack even shelter from the rain. Help us not to rest until your will is done on earth as in heaven.

The Word of God

The Old Testament book of Jonah is a meditation on the absurdity of some of the chosen people's belief that God's love for them was exclusive. Some strands of Judaism interpreted God's choice to form covenant relationship with Israel as an indication that God loved *only* the Jewish people, and that other peoples (the "Gentiles" or "nations" of the Hebrew scriptures) were outside the pale of salvation.

The author of Jonah satirizes such exclusivist notions of salvation. God sends Jonah to preach to the Ninevites, and because he regards them as irreformable, he refuses to go. Nineveh was the capital city of Assyria, an exceedingly cruel military empire. When Jonah resists God's call, God causes one calamity after another to befall him, until Jonah simply gives up and sits down under a gourd vine. The vine withers. Then the epiphanic moment of the narrative occurs: God points out that Jonah grieves because the gourd vine that had sheltered him had withered. Then God tells Jonah that his pity for a vine he had not even planted is but a shadow of God's own pity for the great city of Nineveh: *"And should I not be concerned about Nineveh, that great city, in which there are more than a hundred and twenty thousand persons who do not know their right hand from their left, and also many animals?"* (Jonah 4:11).

Prayer Response

Lord of all nations and cities, no one escapes your compassion. Your glance of mercy scrutinizes our streets full of homeless persons. You see those we pass by and do not see. You see them as persons, not nameless statistics. Your compassion yearns for the wholeness and liberation of each of us. Each comes from your hand; each has incalculable value. Each has priceless gifts we all need to live fuller, more joyous lives.

Merciful Lord, *you* suffer neglect when any human being suffers neglect. You hunger with the hungry, thirst with the thirsty, feel the pain of abuse with the abused. Enlarge our hearts so that we may love the homeless as you love them. Deepen our vision so that we may see those whom we pass without seeing, and above all that we may see you in them.

The Word of God

When the Son of Man comes in his glory, and all the angels with him, then he will sit on the throne of his glory. All the nations will be gathered before him, and he will separate people one from another as a shepherd separates the sheep from the goats, and he will put the sheep at his right hand and the goats at the left. Then the king will say to those at his right hand, "Come, you that are blessed by my Father, inherit the kingdom prepared for you from the foundation of the world: for I was hungry and you gave me food, I was thirsty and you gave me something to drink, I was a stranger and you welcomed me, I was naked and you gave me clothing, I was sick and you took care of me, I was in prison and you visited me." Then the righteous will answer him, "Lord, when was it that we saw you hungry and gave you food, or thirsty and gave you something to drink? And when was it that we saw you a stranger and welcomed you, or naked and gave you clothing. And when was it that we saw you sick or in prison and visited you?" And the king will answer them, "Truly I tell you, just as you did it to one of the least of these who are members of my family, you did it to me" (Matthew 25:31-40).

Prayer Response

Lord, your words have terrible clarity.
We would avoid them if we could.
But their simplicity strikes our hearts.
Let your presence in all homeless persons
Strike our hearts as well.
Lord, help us to see.

Prayers from the Religions of the World

Mother Teresa of Calcutta

> Make us worthy, Lord,
> To serve our brothers and sisters
> Throughout the world who live and die
> In poverty or hunger.
>
> Give them, through our hands,
> their daily bread,
> And by our understanding love,
> Give peace and joy.[8]

*   *   *

Alcuin of York

> When you sit happy in your own fair house,
> Remember all poor folk that are abroad,
> That Christ, who gave this roof, prepare for thee
> Eternal dwelling in the house of God.[9]

*   *   *

George Appleton

> O thou Source of Love and Compassion
> in the sufferings of all thy children,
> we offer our compassion also
> for the hungry, and the sick in body, mind or heart,
> the depressed and the lonely,

---

8. George Appleton, ed., *The Oxford Book of Prayer* (NY: Oxrford UP, 1985), 75-8.
9. Ibid., 135.

all living in fear and under stress,
all stricken in grief,
the unemployed and the rejected,
and those burning with hatred.
Strengthen us to work for their healing
and inspire us to build with thee
the Kingdom of love
where none shall cause suffering to others
and all be caring, loving children of thine,
Our Compassionate, all-embracing Father,
everpresent, everloving,
never failing.[10]

*   *   *

Walter Rauschenbusch

O God, we remember with pain and pity the thousands of our brothers and sisters who seek honest work and seek in vain. For though the unsatisfied wants of men [and women] are many, and though our land is wide and calls for labor, yet these thy sons and daughters have no place to labor, and are turned away in humiliation and despair when they seek it. O righteous God, we acknowledge our common guilt for the disorder of our industry which thrusts even willing workers into the degradation of idleness and want, and teaches some to love the sloth which once they feared and hated.

We remember also with sorrow and compassion the idle rich, who have vigor of body and mind and yet produce no useful thing. Forgive them for loading the burden of their support on the bent shoulders of the working world. Forgive them for wasting in refined excess what would feed the pale children of the poor. Forgive them for setting their poisoned splendor before the thirsty hearts of the young, luring them to theft or shame by the lust of

---

10.   George Appleton, *One Man's Prayers* (London: SPCK, 1967), 52.

eye and flesh. Forgive them for taking pride in their workless lives and despising those by whose toil they live. Forgive them for appeasing their better self by pretended duties and injurious charities. We beseech thee to awaken them by the new voice of thy Spirit that they may look up into the stern eyes of thy Christ and may be smitten with the blessed pangs of repentance. Grant them strength of soul to rise from their silken shame and to give their brothers [and sisters] a just return of labor for the bread they eat. And to our whole nation do thou grant wisdom to create a world in which none shall be forced to idle in want, and none shall be able to idle in luxury, but in which all shall know the health of wholesome work and the sweetness of well-earned rest.[11]

* * *

Basil Naylor

Holy Spirit, fountain of light and truth, help us to understand the causes of our social tensions and unrest. Open our eyes to economic wrongs and racial bias; deepen our concern for the poor, the old, and the handicapped; and stir in us all a burning sense of responsibility one for another, as servants of Jesus Christ our Lord.[12]

* * *

Yom Kippur Morning Service

Remember our brethren [and sisters] of the whole House of Israel, and gather the homeless of our people from the lands of their dispersion. Enable them to return in dignity to Zion, Thy city, and Jerusalem, the dwelling-place of Thy glory. Thus shall be fulfilled the promise set forth in Thy Torah: 'Though your dispersed be in the ends of the earth, from there will the Lord God

---

11. Walter Rauschenbusch, *Prayers of the Social Awakening* (Boston: Pilgrim, 1909), 101-2.
12. Frank Colquhoun, comp. and ed., *Contemporary Parish Prayers* (London: Hodder & Stoughton, 1975), #337.

gather them and bring them into the land which their fathers inherited, and they shall possess it.[13]

*   *   *

W.E.B. DuBois

Let us remember tonight those who are in the bonds of poverty
who have neither sufficient food nor drink, the beauty of home or
the love of beauty. Bring us the day, O God, when the world shall
no longer know such poverty as stunts growth and feeds crime,
and teach us to realize that such things are not necessary to earth
but are the result of our greed and selfishness, our wastefulness
and willful forgetting.[14]

*   *   *

David Adam

You are the caller
You are the poor
You are the stranger at my door

You are the wanderer
The unfed
You are the homeless
With no bed

You are the man
Driven insane
You are the child
Crying in pain

You are the other who comes to me
If I open to another you're born in me.[15]

---

13.   Rabbi Morris Silverman, comp., *High Holiday Prayer Book* (Bridgeport, CT:
Prayer Book Press, 1986), 320.
14.   W.E.B. DuBois, *Prayers for a Dark People*, ed. Herbert Aptheker (Amherst: Univ.
of Massachusetts, 1980), 49.

Actions on Behalf of Justice for the Homeless

Some churches and parishes have organized study groups to learn about homelessness. In their study and discussion sessions, such groups can pay particular attention to the *causes* of homelessness: why do people in our country become homeless today? Who are among the homeless? What are the links between homelessness and economic injustice, or homelessness and unemployment?

Excellent resources for study include Bard, *Shadow Women,* a set of first-person narratives by homeless women; and Kozol, *Rachel and Her Children.*

* * *

A study group could organize lectures for both the church and the community. Resource persons who could be brought in for such lectures might be community activists who have organized outreach programs for the homeless, pastors who have organized programs to confront homelessness in their churches, and university professors who address the problem of homelessness in the classroom. For other suggestions about resource people, you may consider contacting any person or group in your area whose primary ministry is working with homeless persons.

* * *

Churches and parishes around the country are organizing soup kitchens to feed homeless persons. If your church is not similarly involved, you could help organize a soup kitchen. If such a project is already underway, you might work in a soup kitchen. A resource group for information about such an activity is Catholic Worker, which has branches in many American cities. Its national address is 36 E. 1st St., New York, NY 10003; (212) 254-1640.

Questions to consider if you involve yourself in soup-kitchen work: how can those who feed the homeless move to action that

---

15. David Adam, *The Edge of Glory: Prayers in the Celtic Tradition* (London: SPCK, 1985), 34.

does not merely alleviate the problem, but addresses its root causes. How can those feeding the homeless avoid a patronizing attitude toward those they serve? How does one move from merely dispensing charity to acquiring an effective knowledge of those whom one feeds?

Dom Helder Câmara, a Brazilian cardinal, says that when he feeds the hungry, people call him a saint. When he asks why anyone is hungry, people call him a communist. What does he mean by this? How does this statement challenge us to move beyond band-aid activism to work for systemic change?

*   *   *

Homelessness is a political issue. Economic planning at the national level either exacerbates the problem of homelessness or addresses it positively. A number of groups monitor congressional voting patterns with regard to issues such as care for the homeless. You may consider joining such a group; two such groups are the Center of Concern, 3700 13th Street, Washington, DC 20017; (202) 635-2757; and Network, 806 Rhode Island Ave. NE, Washington, DC 20018; (202) 526-4070.

In addition, you may write your congresspersons to ask their views on the problem of homelessness. If you consider their position to be one of unconcern, challenge them to take a more effective stand. Make available to others information rating the performance of your political representatives in the area of concern for the homeless.

*   *   *

A number of church or parish study groups have invited a homeless person to address them. If you consider doing this, a good way to set up such a meeting might be by contacting one of the resource persons mentioned above—particularly a pastor or religious whose primary concern is with the homeless. Among the benefits of inviting a homeless person to address your group would be that you could hear about the experience of homelessness first-hand, and you would have the opportunity to become acquainted with a homeless *person*.

A drawback of extending such an invitation is the possibility that your groups might unintentionally exploit the person invited. Forms of exploitation could include using the person to make one-self feel sentimentally good about one's concern for the homeless; or assuming that one contact makes one "know" the homeless person. If you decide to invite a homeless person to address your group, then, it would be necessary to pay attention to what resource people might tell you about avoiding patronizing attitudes as you invite and listen to a homeless person.

*   *   *

The laws of your local community or city probably have many important effects on the homeless in your area. Activists in many communities have organized to protest the unavailability of low-cost housing for the poor; they seek legislative change that will enable the poor to buy houses more easily. You can consider joining such organized activity, or organizing one in your own community.

If you do this, seek first to inform yourself about your city's laws regarding unused housing, home ownership, the homeless, etc. Then focus your actions on changing the particular laws in your community that work against the needs of homeless persons.

A group that works to provide affordable and decent housing for the poor is Habitat for Humanity, whose national address is Habitat and Church Sts., Americus, GA 31709-3498; (912) 924-7776.

*   *   *

In recent decades, a significant number of homeless people in America are those discharged prematurely from mental health institutions. In studying the problem of homelessness, you should inform yourself about the growing problem of inadequate mental health care.

A helpful resource for this is Harrington, *New American Poverty*, especially Chapter 5. Why are so many people who need institutional treatment homeless on our streets?

*   *   *

Most cities with a homeless population have some program to pick up the homeless on nights when the temperature falls below freezing. If such a program does not exist in your city, you may consider organizing it. If there is such a program, you may participate in it. In either case, you may wish to contact local Salvation Army groups for more information.

*   *   *

Resources for Further Study

Bard, Marjorie. *Shadow Women: Homeless Women's Survival Stories*. Kansas City: Sheed & Ward, 1990.

Harrington, Michael. *The New American Poverty*. New York: Holt, Rinehart and Winston, 1984.

Kozol, Jonathan. *Rachel and Her Children: Homeless Families in America*. New York: Fawcett/Columbine, 1988.

Chapter Two
Ona, A Single Mother

The Imaginative Journey

I had my first baby when I was sixteen.

Mama married once. Callie and Hawkins were by Mr. Albert Simmons, her husband. He left. Then she had Florette and me by our daddy, Leo Clemson, and Sabrina by another man. We never knew his name. She wouldn't say.

Mama worked sometimes. She never finished high school, so she got jobs cleaning houses and offices. The last job was at night. One night when she was cleaning a building, a man got inside and held a knife to her throat and raped her.

All these jobs paid minimum wage, no benefits. Even with food stamps, Mama couldn't always feed us and pay rent. We lived in a two-bedroom subsidized apartment. The walls had roaches, and sometimes they climbed on the baby in the crib. We ate lots of rice and beans and cereal.

It was easier to draw welfare.

Mama made us go to church. She tried to raise us right. But seemed like half the folks in the apartment project did drugs. Lots of times teenagers would get together in the halls to smoke or shoot up; men who sold the stuff would cruise the projects looking for someone to sell to. Where there are drugs, there's killing. I once saw a fourteen-year-old boy shot in the stomach outside the building. He crumpled and moaned and looked kind of surprised. He was scared. He died.

Mama tried to keep us away from all that meanness. The hardest thing was to keep men away from us girls. Mama's last boyfriend, Slim Rogers, stayed with us at night, and one night when Mama was at work he tried to force me. I ran outside. When Mama found out about that, she broke up with him.

I met Al when I was fourteen. He was different; he didn't fool with drugs and made good grades in school. What was nice was that we could go on the bus downtown and have a good time without much money. We would just look in the windows and watch people on the street. Al could make anything seem funny. He made me feel special.

When I knew I was pregnant, Al wanted to quit school and work to help me and the baby. I didn't want him to. For awhile we still saw each other, but before the baby was born Al and his mother moved away. I think maybe he was glad to leave. I never hear from him.

Mama was good with my little girl Doreen. I got a job at a hamburger place to help out. Then I slipped near the grill in the restaurant and hit my head. They told me they didn't have insurance to help pay my medical bills. I got an x-ray, but the doctors didn't think I needed treatment. Sometimes my head still aches and I get dizzy.

I had Donald, Jr., when I was eighteen. This time I didn't really love my baby's daddy. It just happened. Now, I draw welfare like Mama. Most days I sit home with Doreen and Donald, Jr. In the middle of summer, we can hardly stand the heat and flies. Only one window in the apartment has a screen that's not torn. We have to close the windows at night even when it's hot, to keep people from trying to get in. Next door the man and woman who live there with three kids fight and carry on all day long. When he's not hitting her or she's not throwing something at him, they play the radio so loud that Donald, Jr., cries most of the day.

Mama goes out to do housework; the ladies she works for don't report this, so she can draw her welfare and work at the same time.

I want something more for my kids.

Scriptural Reflections

The Word of God

In the beginning when God created the heavens and the earth, the earth was a formless void and darkness covered the face of the deep, while a wind from God swept over the face of the waters. Then God said, "Let there be light"; and there was light. And God saw that the light was good; and God separated the light from the darkness (Genesis 1:1-2).

Prayer Response

Lord our maker, maker of all, your spirit births creation by brooding over it like a mother bird on its nest. We justly name you our divine Mother; you watch over us and yearn for our good with the tenderness of a mother for her children.

Keep us mindful of the many mothers in our midst who struggle to feed their children. Make us aware of the obstacles our societies place in the path of these mothers as they strive to raise children with dignity and hope. Help us to understand and not judge; give us hands to help and not push away.

We commit ourselves to solidarity with all women everywhere, as they seek to cast off the shackles of historic oppression. We commit ourselves to their quest for justice and bread, for themselves and their families.

The Word of God

In the sixth month the angel Gabriel was sent by God to a town in Galilee called Nazareth, to a virgin engaged to a man whose name was Joseph, of the house of David. The virgin's name was Mary. And he came to her and said, "Greetings, favored one! The Lord is with you." But she was much perplexed by his words and pondered what sort of greeting this might be. The angel said to her, "Do not be afraid, Mary, for you have found favor with God. And now, you will conceive in your womb and bear a son, and you will name him Jesus, the Son of the Most High, and the Lord God will give to him the throne of his ancestor David. He will reign over the house of Jacob forever, and of his kingdom there will be no end." Mary said to the angel, "How can this be, since I am a virgin?" (Luke 1:26-34).

Now the birth of Jesus the Messiah took place in this way. When his mother Mary had been engaged to Joseph, but before they had lived to-

gether, she was found to be with child from the Holy Spirit. Her husband Joseph, being a righteous man and unwilling to expose her to public disgrace, planned to dismiss her quietly. But just when he had resolved to do this, an angel of the Lord appeared to him in a dream and said, "Joseph, son of David, do not be afraid to take Mary as your wife, for the child conceived in her is from the Holy Spirit" (Matthew 1:18-20).

Prayer Response

Lord, our faith roots itself in the astonishing *fiat*, the "let it be done," of your mother. When the good news of your coming was announced to her, she opened herself completely and without reservation to God's will.

We recall what Mary risked by her act of faith. She risked being branded a loose woman, excluded by her family and her society. She risked the incomprehension of Joseph her betrothed. Already in her conception of you the shadow of the cross fell across her life. The road to Calvary led from Nazareth.

As we meditate on Mary's act of faith, help us to see more clearly the web of destructive social realities in which the single mother finds herself caught. Help us not to stigmatize, but to change those structures of our society that contribute to single motherhood.

We accept your challenge to choose life. Let our choice for life be resolute and wide-reaching. If we commit ourselves to oppose abortion, let us also commit ourselves to oppose those ugly social handicaps that drive so many desperate women to choose abortion. If we commit ourselves to saving the lives of unborn children, let us also commit ourselves to eradicating all threats to life, including economic injustice, exploitation of women and other marginal persons, and the beast of war in whose belly we live at this moment of history.

The Word of God

The scribes and Pharisees brought a woman who had been caught in adultery; and making her stand before all of them, they said to him, "Teacher, this woman was caught in the very act of committing adultery. Now in the law Moses commanded us to stone such women. Now what do you say?" They said this to test him, so that they might have some charge to bring against him. Jesus bent down and wrote with his finger on the ground. *When they kept on questioning him, he straightened up and said to them, "Let anyone among you who is without sin be the first to throw a stone at her." And once again he bent down and wrote on the ground. When they heard it, they went away, one by one, beginning with the elders; and Jesus was left alone with the woman standing before him. Jesus straightened up and said to her, "Woman, where are they? Has no one condemned you?" She said, "No one, sir." And Jesus said, "Neither do I condemn you. Go your way, and from now on do not sin again"* (John 8:3-11).

Prayer Response

Lord, when the adulterous woman was brought before you, you indicated your unconcern with condemnation by doodling on the ground. Fill our hearts with your compassion. Against your culture's practice, you invited women to be your disciples. You commended Martha's sister Mary for pondering your words, not for cooking and cleaning. You initiated a theological conversation with the Samaritan woman, an outcast as both a woman and a Samaritan. Among your disciples, it was Mary Magdalene who foresaw your approaching death and anointed your feet as you walked to death. It was the women among your followers who followed you to Calvary, and the women who first witnessed your resurrection. Help us to walk in your footsteps by living in solidarity with all women everywhere who yearn for a better existence.

Prayers from the Religions of the World

Ethiopian Orthodox Hymn

O Lord, remember thy descent from the heights of Heaven and thine indwelling within the womb of the Holy Virgin.

Remember thy birth from her while she was a virgin, and the suckling of her who wast chaste.

Remember how thou wast laid in a manger, wrapped in swaddling clothes, in a stable.

O Lord remembering all this, do not disregard thy sinful servant. Help me with thy deliverance and cover me with the shield of thy salvation for the sake of Mary thy Mother; for the sake of her breasts which suckled thee and her lips which kissed thee; for the sake of her hands which touched thee and her arms which embraced thee; for the sake of her spirit and flesh which thou didst take from her to be part of thyself.[16]

*　　　*　　　*

Ramanuja

Thou my mother, and my father thou,
Thou my friend, and my teacher thou.
Thou my wisdom, and my riches thou.
Thou art all to me, O God of all gods.[17]

*　　　*　　　*

Walter Rauschenbusch

From the fear of unemployment and the evils of overwork, from the curse of child-labor and the ill-paid toil of women, Good Lord, deliver us.[18]

*　　　*　　　*

Indian Christian prayer

Dear Jesus, as a hen covers her chicks with her wings to keep them safe, do thou this dark night protect us under your golden wing.[19]

*　　　*　　　*

---

16. *Oxford Book of Prayer*, 251-3.
17. Ibid., 286.
18. *Prayers of Social Awakening*, 121.
19. *Oxford Book of Prayer*, 124.

W.E.B. Dubois

Give us grace, O God, to dare to do the deed which we well know cries to be done. Let us not hesitate because of ease, or the words of men's [and women's] mouths, or our own lives. Mighty causes are calling us—the freeing of women, the training of children, the putting down of hate and murder and poverty—all these and more. But they call with voices that mean work and sacrifice and death. Mercifully grant us, O God, the spirit of Esther, that we say: I will go unto the King and if I perish, I perish—Amen.[20]

Actions on Behalf of Justice for Single Mothers

Parishes and churches across the country have study groups to raise the consciousness of church members about social issues such as single motherhood. If your church or parish does not have such a group, you might organize one to investigate the social factors leading to single motherhood. Pay particular attention to how such problems as lack of adequate jobs, decent housing, and good education contribute to single motherhood.

A good starting point for study is Harrington, *New American Poverty*, especially Chapter 8. Other good resources include Neu and Riley, *Women Moving Church*; and Burke, *Reaching for Justice*.

*   *   *

Government policies have a great deal to do with whether women receive adequate wages for their work, whether the welfare system operates fairly and to the advantage of impoverished children, and whether adequate housing and education are available for all Americans. Many groups monitor the voting patterns of Congress; such groups advocate writing your congresspersons to urge them to support programs that assure good jobs, education, assistance to poor women, etc.

---

20. *Prayers for a Dark People*, 21.

You might consider joining such a group: two groups are the Center of Concern and Network, references to which are in the *Actions* list of Journey I. Also, think about writing your congresspersons to ask about their views on women's issues. Publicize what you learn of their voting record with regard to issues affecting the well-being of women.

*   *   *

Most communities have shelters for battered women, or crisis lines that provide assistance and information to women who are being beaten by their partners. You may wish to volunteer to participate in such work. You can usually contact women's centers by looking in your telephone information pages under such headings as "Crisis Line," or "Women's Resource Centers."

*   *   *

Activists and pastors or religious who work with the poor often organize demonstrations to call for better welfare benefits and reform of the welfare system. The laws that make it easier for single-parent families to obtain assistance than for those with two parents are in need of reform; these laws contribute to the disintegration of welfare families. You may think about participating in such demonstrations, or organizing one in your community.

*   *   *

Another cause that receives attention in many communities is that of education. You may wish to participate in a lobbying effort for better funding for public education in your local area and around the nation. Demand that standards for teachers be more stringent, that good teachers be rewarded, and that wages be sufficient to insure that highly qualified persons continue to enter the profession.

*   *   *

In recent years, social activists have tracked the growth of an alarming marketing pattern in some major corporations. Some companies that sell food products have begun to dump inferior or dangerous products on third-world markets. In some cases, the targeted market is specifically infants or children in third-world countries. These inferior or dangerous products have been shown to damage the health of third-world children, even to cause death.

You may want to study this problem and involve yourself in a group that monitors the distribution and marketing policies of corporations selling infant products in third-world countries. Such a group is the Council on Economic Priorities, 30 Irving Place, New York, NY 10003; (212) 420-1133. If the marketing policies of corporations fail to protect the health of infants, participate in boycotts and protests.

* * *

Various community-service organizations have programs in which sponsors "adopt" a single mother. Your city or town may have such a program. To find out about this, you can contact social welfare agencies or women's service organizations in your community.

If you "adopt" a single mother and she has not finished high school, encourage and help her to do so. Assist her in finding an adequate job and adequate housing.

* * *

You may wish to plan or sponsor a series of presentations in your church or parish on the problem of sexual abuse of children. Others who have done this recommend that you invite speakers from the social services, psychiatric, and legal profession who are informed about the problem. Ask your speakers to help your group probe the underlying social causes of this problem.

* * *

You may decide to subscribe to a publication providing information about the struggle of women to achieve equality in the workplace. Co-Op America's journal, *Building Economic Alternatives*, is one such publication. You may subscribe to it by joining Co-Op America, whose address is 2100 M Street, N.W., #310, Washington, DC 20063; (202) 872-5307.

*   *   *

During Women's History Month (March), on International Women's Day (March 8), or on Mother's Day, church and parish groups around the world sponsor prayer vigils to express concerns from all of the above activities. You may consider organizing such a vigil. If so, seek to raise the consciousness of the community in which you live or worship regarding the needs and concerns of women.

Some resources helpful for organizing such a liturgical celebration include Chittister, *WomanStrength*; and Kirk, *Celebration of Biblical Women's Stories*.

*   *   *

Resources for Further Study

Burke, Mary. *Reaching for Justice: The Women's Movement.* Washington, DC: Center of Concern, 1980.

Chittister, Joan. *WomanStrength: Modern Church, Modern Women.* Kansas City: Sheed & Ward, 1990.

Harrington, Michael. *The New American Poverty.* New York: Holt, Rinehart and Winston, 1984.

Kirk, Martha Ann. *Celebration of Biblical Women's Stories.* Kansas City: Sheed & Ward, 1989.

Neu, Dianne and Maria Riley. *Women Moving Church.* Washington, DC: Center of Concern, 1982.

Chapter Three

Julio Léon, A Campesino

The Imaginative Journey

I, Julio Léon Salazar, am a *campesino*.

My grandfathers and grandmothers lived on this land. Their grandfathers and grandmothers did as well. They had little plots of land and grew food for their families—vegetables, beans, goats, a few chickens. There was never a great deal to eat, but usually enough.

In my grandfather's lifetime a *patrón* took over the land and rented it to the *campesinos*. No one understood how he got the right to do this. But we live far from the capital city where such things are decided.

In my father's lifetime, the *patrón* sold the land to a coffee company. American businessmen own the company. We no longer grow our food on the land. We work for a wage. Everything is coffee.

The overseers call us animals. They tell us that we are stupid like animals. They say we do not have minds, only strong arms and backs to cultivate coffee. They work us like animals.

Work begins every day at dawn. My wife is up before dawn to cook bread on the griddle. She mashes the beans from supper and they are my breakfast, with the bread. On rare occasions there is some fat pork as well.

Then I go to the coffee groves. We work till mid-morning and the overseer allows us a break. Then we eat the bread and beans our wives have sent with us. We are always hungry in mid-morning, so the food tastes good. Then we go back to work. Lunch is rice and beans again. We are happy to have food. Many people in our country do not have this much to eat.

The afternoon is the hardest time. In the old days, people took siestas. When the weather is hot, it is refreshing to take a siesta. The overseer does so, but if he found us sleeping, he would fire us. He tells us that we have to work for our living, and that privileges belong to those who are our superiors. He tells us that God has arranged it that way, and to question this arrangement is to question God.

We talk among ourselves when we are free to do so.

By night I am always near a stupor. To work at the same tasks every day, eat the same meager food every day, without hope of having a better life, makes me sometimes think that the overseer is right: I am an animal. But when I begin to think this, a voice inside me says no, I am not a brute creature. I am a human being.

The best nights are when we can drink. We still have some fiestas, but they are not like the ones about which my father and mother told stories. In the old days there were many fiestas. On fiestas there would be no work for several days. The village would cook together; we would slaughter our goats or pigs and the whole village would cook them in pits. The women would prepare special dishes together. On the day of the fiesta, everyone would eat and eat, and the men would drink.

Now the overseer tells us that the owners of the plantation do not want fiestas. Fiestas are a symbol of the laziness and backwardness of *campesinos*, he tells us. So we have only a few fiestas. The best thing about them is that we can drink and not worry about getting up to work early the next day.

It is hard to fit my whole family into my house. We have six children living. My wife has borne ten children, but four died as babies. In summer there are always fevers, and babies die easily from them. When a baby dies no one grieves for long. We hope that some of our children will live and be well so that someone can take care of us when we can no longer work. My wife washes clothes for the Americans in the town. She sometimes brings home magazines about North America. The pictures are beautiful.

They make us think that there can be a better life. To have electric lights and running water. . . .

We worry about being sick or growing old. When you become sick, you cannot work. When you cannot work, you do not eat. Several years ago, I hurt my back lifting a heavy hamper of coffee beans. I could not work for several weeks. An old woman in the village knows how to cure; she put hot compresses of leaves wrapped in cloth on my back, and it got better. But there are still days when the pain is great.

My wife prays. We have holy pictures and candles in the house. But church is for those who have money. Does God hear the prayers of those who toil like animals?

Once on a national fiesta, I took my oldest son with me to the capital city. We went to Mass in the cathedral. At communion time, the priests came down the aisle among the people. Ahead of me in the line for communion was another *campesino*. The priest questioned him and would not give him communion. When he came to me, I stood before him. He did not even see me. I am sorry for my son to see this happen to me.

A group of sisters has opened a school for children of the coffee workers. This happened before and the government closed it. They said that the sisters were political activists and not religious. We hope that the school will remain open this time. The sisters have organized prayer circles. Those who go tell me that the sisters say we are God's children, God has a special love for the poor, and the Bible does not tell God's children to be content with injustice. The sisters say that God wants us to work for a better world. This is what we have often said among ourselves when the overseer was not listening. But to think this way is difficult: it invites trouble from the company owners and the government.

I would like to see a better world, one with enough for everybody to eat, with work that does not kill the worker, with houses large enough for all the children.

I sometimes have a dream. In it the whole world is like a fiesta.

Scriptural Reflections

The Word of God

Then God said, "Let us make humankind in our image, according to our likeness; and let them have dominion over the fish of the sea, and over the birds of the air, and over the cattle, and over all the wild animals of the earth, and over every creeping thing that creeps upon the earth." So God created humankind in his image, in the image of God he created them; male and female he created them. God blessed them, and God said to them, "Be fruitful and multiply, and fill the earth and subdue it; and have dominion over the fish of the sea and over the birds of the air and over every living thing that moves upon the earth." God said, "See, I have given you every plant yielding seed that is upon the face of all the earth, and every tree with seed in its fruit; you shall have them for food. And to every beast of the earth, and to every bird of the air, and to everything that creeps on the earth, everything that has the breath of life, I have given every green plant for food" (Genesis 1:26-30).

Prayer Response

Gracious God, all things come from your hand. All that comes from you is good and life-giving. In your wonderful love, you give the earth itself into our hands, so that we may share in your creative work.

We who image you are one family, all born of your creative love. We who share the earth are one family. You give it to us all alike. It is your will that all eat of the good things of the earth and bless your name.

Your will be done on earth as in heaven. When we address you as our Father, our Mother, we remember that we speak in union with all the peoples of the earth—you are *our* parent, the creator of *all*.

Many of the people of our earth are hungry, jobless, oppressed, lacking adequate medical care. These evils exist not according to your will, but through human indifference, cruelty, and greed—*our* indifference, cruelty, and greed.

We dare to call you our Father, our Mother. This means that we commit ourselves to the task of building a just and peaceful world, in which *all* can partake of the good things of the earth. *Then* your name will be hallowed on earth as in heaven.

The Word of God

Ah, you who join house to house, who add field to feild, until there is room for no one but you, and you are left to live alone in the midst of the land! The Lord of hosts has sworn in my hearing: Surely many houses shall be desolate, large and beautiful houses, without inhabitant. For ten acres of vineyard shall yield but one bath, and a homer of seed shall yield a mere ephah (Isaiah 5:8-9).

Prayer Response

Lord, you burn with anger at human greed. You look at what we have made of your good earth, and grieve that so few monopolize the good things of the world and so many are excluded from enjoying them. You pledge yourself to overturn this unrighteous situation, in which the few hoard what you gave to all.

We confess our guilt; we fear your righteous anger, because we share in the sin of adding house to house and field to field, so that we have more than we need and others do not have the bare necessities of life. We confess our society's guilt before you: we live in that region of the planet that consumes most of the world's goods and that uses the rest of the world to supply its luxuries. We know that we carry the burden of a social sin you oppose, a sin you will root out.

As we ask forgiveness, we commit ourselves to your cause. We wish to join with you in overturning injustice and effecting justice. We give you our hands, so that with them the old structures of greed may be dismantled, and new structures of justice be built. We give you our hands, so that the bread you give us may be shared with all who need.

The Word of God

A shoot shall come out from the stump of Jesse, and a branch shall grow out of his roots. The spirit of the Lord shall rest on him, the spirit of wisdom and understanding, the spirit of counsel and might, the spirit of knowledge and the fear of the Lord. His delight shall be in the fear of the Lord. He shall not judge by what his eyes see, or decide by what his ears hear; but with righteousness he shall judge the poor, and decide with equ-

ity for the meek of the earth; he shall strike the earth with the rod of his mouth, and with the breath of his lips he shall kill the wicked. Righteousness shall be the belt around his waist, and faithfulness the belt around his loins. The wolf shall live with the lamb, the leopard shall lie down with the kid, the calf and the lion and the fatling together, and a little child shall lead them (Isaiah 11:1-6).

Prayer Response

Lord Jesus, you announced the coming reign of God. You proclaimed this reign as the rule of justice. You preached that in God's reign the poor would be blessed and the mighty mourn.

With you, we dream of the fulfillment of all the rich promise of the earth. We long for the day when the oppressor will be judged with justice and the ruthless struck down. We await with joyous expectation the day in which the lion and the lamb shall lie down together. We call you Lord: we commit ourselves to the task of building this reign of justice and peace in our broken world.

The Word of God

Then he looked up at his disciples and said: "Blessed are you who are poor, for yours is the kingdom of God. Blessed are you who are hungry now, for you will be filled. Blessed are you who weep now, for you will laugh. Blessed are you when people hate you, and when they exclude you, revile you, and defame you on account of the Son of Man. Rejoice in that day and leap for joy, for surely your reward is great in heaven; for that is what their ancestors did to the prophets. But woe to you who are rich, for you have received your consolation. Woe to you who are full now, for you will be hungry. Woe to you who are laughing now, for you will mourn and weep. Woe to you when all speak well of you, for that is what their ancestors did to the false prophets" (Luke 6:20-26).

Prayer Response

Lord, you have the words of everlasting life. We hear your words and we tremble before their judgment. We welcome your words because in them is our liberation.

The Word of God

There was a rich man who was dressed in purple and fine linen and who feasted sumptuously every day. And at his gate lay a poor man named Lazarus, covered with sores, who longed to satisfy his hunger with what fell from the rich man's table; even the dogs would come and lick his sores. The poor man died and was carried away by the angels to be with Abraham. The rich man also died and was buried. In Hades, he looked up and saw Abraham far away with Lazarus by his side. He called out, "Father Abraham, have mercy on me, and send Lazarus to dip the tip of his finger in water and cool my tongue; for I am in agony in these flames." But Abraham said, "Child, remember that during your lifetime, you received your good things, and Lazarus in like manner evil things; but now he is comforted here, and you are in agony. Besides all this, between you and us a great chasm has been fixed, so that those who might want to pass from here to you cannot do so, and no one can cross from there to us." He said, "Then, father, I beg you to send him to my father's house—for I have five brothers—that he may warn them, so that they will not also come into this place of torment." Abraham replied, "They have Moses and the prophets; they should listen to them." He said, "No, father Abraham; but if someone goes to them from the dead, they will repent." He said to him, "If they do not listen to Moses and the prophets, neither will they be convinced even if someone rises from the dead" (Luke 16:19-31).

Prayer Response

As we ponder your word, Lord, we see that *we* are the rich man of the parable. Lazarus lives in the vast portions of the globe in which most human beings barely keep body and soul together. Lazarus lies at our gate. We see him on our television sets at night, as we eat our evening meals and turn on the news. He starves in the third-world baby as we throw away our leftovers, or as we skimp because we are overweight, overfed and underworked.

Open our eyes so that we can truly see the world in which we live, so that we can recognize our complicity in making and keeping the world as it us. Keep us from resting easy with this world. Keep telling us the story of the rich man and Lazarus.

Prayers from the Religions of the World

Walter Rauschenbusch

O God, thou Father of us all, we praise thee that thou hast bound humanity in a great unity of life so that each must lean on the strength of all, and depend for his [and her] comfort and safety on the help and labor of his brothers [and sisters].

We invoke thy blessing on all the men and women who have toiled to build and warm our homes, to fashion our raiment, and to wrest from sea and land the food that nourishes us and our children.

We pray that they may have health and joy, and hope and love, even as we desire for our own loved ones.

Grant us wisdom to deal justly and fraternally with every man and woman whom we face in the business of life.

May we not unknowingly inflict suffering through selfish indifference or the wilful ignorance of a callous heart.

Since the comforts of our life are brought to us from afar, and made by those whom we do not know or see, grant us organized intelligence and power that we may send the command of our righteous will along the channels of trade and industry, and help to cleanse them of hardness and unfairness.

May the time come when we need wear and use nothing that is wet in thy sight with human tears, or cheapened by wearing down the lives of the weak.

Save us, we beseech thee, from unconscious guilt.

Speak thou to our souls and bid us strive for the coming of thy kingdom of justice when thy merciful and saving will shall be done on earth.[21]

*   *   *

Abbé Raynal

In the eighteenth century, a French priest, Abbé Raynal, describ-ed conditions on French sugar cane plantations in the West Indies. Raynal visited some of these plantations and was shocked at the brutality of the slave system by which sugar was produced, by the great misery inflicted on some human beings so that Europeans might have the luxury of sugar.

He reflected on a curious fact: the citizens of Paris crowded the theaters of the city and wept copiously over the tragedies enacted on stage. But they never shed tears over the real sufferings of the slaves who supplied them with sugar. Raynal concluded, "The torments of a people to whom we owe our luxuries never seem to reach our hearts."

What Raynal has to say seems to apply to us today. Many of the luxuries we consume are bought at the heavy price of exploita-tion. The price we pay for our luxuries is often the oppression of the third-world worker (or the worker in marginated areas of our own country): wages that cannot sustain workers and their famil-ies at a level of humane existence, lack of benefits to protect work-ers and their families in sickness or old age, and on and on.

*　　　*　　　*

W.D. Lindsey

We sip our morning coffee to come alive.
We put our mug on the table and open our Bibles.
"God is love," we read.
"You have been told what is good,
Do good, love the right, and walk humbly with your God."
We sit wrapped in the stillness of the dawntime house,
Praying, thinking, listening to the Lord,
Welcoming life-giving words.

---

21. *Prayers of Social Awakening*, 65-6.

And we relish the good coffee of Latin America,
Africa, the Caribbean,
With the good sugar of Louisiana cane fields.

We pray and we forget.

We forget the bent backs of the coffee workers,
The dejection of the cane harvesters.
They sweat and groan and toil like animals,
And never see the fruits of their labor,
Never glimpse a better life.

God is love.

Lord, stop our lips from glib declarations of your care.
We speak from blindness that will not see.
Let the torments of those to whom we owe our luxuries
Reach our hearts.

Teach us to pray
With all those who groan and toil
To give us our sweet morning coffee, our lettuce,
Our grapes, the coal to heat our houses.

Only then can we dare to pray,
To call you mother, father,
To speak about your love.

*   *   *

Yom Kippur Avodah Service

We corrupt the instruments of state, its powers and its laws by
placing in authority those whose hearts are set upon their gains,
and who, by betraying their trust, give free rein to the tyrannous
instincts of the strong and the cunning.

In accord with today's Avodah, let us purge our common-
wealths of their inherited wrong, and consecrate them to further-
ing the life, the welfare and the virtue of their citizens.

We violate the sacredness of nationhood by allowing it to be
exploited in behalf of greed and oppression, of arrogant dominion

and empire, and by exalting, as its prime purpose and ideal, the waging of war and the spreading of devastation.

In accord with today's Avodah, let us dismiss these cruel ways of the national being into the wasteland of forgotten barbarities, and, by striving to embody it in the Commonwealth of Humanity, dedicate it to the cause of human good. !22

*   *   *

Yom Kippur Evening Service

If one has no mercy for his brother,
How dare he make supplication for his own sins?
Scanty bread is the life of the poor;
He that deprives him thereof is a man of blood.
He slays his neighbor who takes away his living;
And a blood-shedder is he
That deprives the hireling of his wages.
Say not, "If I sin, no eye beholds it,
Or if I deal untruly in all secrecy, who will know it?"
They that lack understanding say these things,
And the man of folly thinks this. !23

*   *   *

The Qur'an Sūra, 2:172-3

It is not piety, that you turn your faces to the East and to the West. True piety is this: to believe in God, and the Last Day, the angels, the Book, and the Prophets, to give of one's substance, however cherished, to one's kin, and orphans, the needy, the traveller, beggars, and to ransom the slave, to perform the prayer, to pay the alms. And they who fulfill their covenant when they have engaged in a covenant, and endure with fortitude misfortune,

---

22. *High Holiday Prayer Book*, 218-30.
23. Ibid., 208-54.

hardship and peril, these are they who are true to their faith, these are the truly godfearing.[24]

Actions on Behalf of Justice for Third-World Workers

Christians ministering in Latin America note that first-world political and economic structures contribute to the plight of the poor there. These ministers urge us to educate ourselves about the political situation in both the first and third world and, in particular, about the interconnections that help to sustain injustice in Latin America. To meet this challenge to raise your consciousness, you might plan a reading project.

An excellent starting point would be Lernoux, *Cry of the People.* Another good resource is *Global Factory,* a study manual prepared by the American Friends' Service Committee, which explores connections between American business decisions and third-world workers. It is available from the Maquiladora Project, Community Relations Division, 1501 Cherry St., Philadelphia, PA 19102 ; (215) 241-7000.

*   *   *

Consumer watchdog groups are studying labor and marketing policies of major American corporations with large third-world interests. These groups and other human-rights organizations note that many American companies pay third-world laborers woefully inadequate wages and provide hardly any job security or benefits for their workers.

If you wish to inform yourself about labor practices of American corporations with third-world interests, two good resources are *Food, Hunger, Agribusiness* and *Human Rights: A Directory of Resources.* Both are available from Third-World Resources, 464 19th St., Oakland, CA 94612; (415) 835-4692. You may also choose to

---

24. *The Koran Interpreted,* trans. A.J. Arberry (London: Unwin Hyman, 1955), Sura 2:172-3).

join the organization Bread for the World, which works for economic justice and a decent standard of living for all world citizens. The address of this group is Bread for the World, World Hunger Association, 802 Rhode Island Avenue, NE, Washington, DC 20018.

*   *   *

Many churches have missionary programs in Latin American countries. You may decide to participate in one of these proggrams. For information about this, you could contact your pastor. Other resources include Maryknoll Missioners, Maryknoll, NY 10545 (a Roman Catholic missionary order), and Witness for Peace, Box 567, Durham, NC 27702 (an interfaith missionary group).

*   *   *

Churches and parishes throughout the country have "adopted" or formed filial relationships with churches and parishes in Latin America. You may consider urging your church to do this. If so, you could explore how to go about it with your pastor, or you might contact the offices of the local governing structure of your church (e.g., in Roman Catholicism, the diocesan offices).

*   *   *

The theological movement called liberation theology is teaching Latin American Christians (and first-world Christians as well) to hear with new ears the liberation message of the Judaeo-Christian scriptures. You may decide to form a church or parish study group to read some key texts of this movement.

Some good texts with which to start include Gutiérrez, *Theology of Liberation*; and Brown, *Theology in a New Key*. It would perhaps help if your group can call on the assistance of a theologian or religion teacher who has some familiarity with this theological movement.

*   *   *

Activists and Christian ministers urge us to write our congresspersons to inquire about their views regarding business practices of multinational corporations. Do our elected representatives have a coherent political program to deal with such problems as the violation or disregard of national labor laws by multinational corporations? Are they concerned about the exploitation of third-world laborers by American-based businesses? You can write your political representatives to find out their stance regarding such issues. Publicize what you discover.

*　　　　　*　　　　　*

One of the most challenging witnesses for social and economic justice in Latin America was the archbishop of San Salvador, Oscar Romero. On March 24, 1980, he was assassinated because of his identification with the oppressed poor people of his country. You may choose to commemorate this martyr's death by planning a prayer vigil in your church. You might accompany the vigil with a public procession. In some communities, such processions witness publicly against first-world exploitation of third-world labor by praying in front of a first-world corporation office or the federal government offices in the community.

*　　　　　*　　　　　*

In recent years, a network of groups has sprung up to offer sanctuary to those fleeing oppression in Central America. Many such refugees will not be granted visas by the United States, even though returning to their country almost certainly will mean torture or death for them. You may consider offering financial or other support to a sanctuary group.

These groups have formed a national alliance from which you may obtain further information. The address is Alliance of Sanctuary Communities/8th Day Center, 1020 S. Wabash Ave., Room 680, Chicago, IL 60605.

*　　　　　*　　　　　*

Developmental psychologists have shown that attitudes of openness or suspicion of the culturally different are formed early in a child's life. Educational programs thus have an important role to play in teaching crosscultural sensitivity and awareness of other cultures. You may decide to see what the schools in your community are doing to teach children about Latin American cultures, and to instill in them attitudes of openness to other cultures. A possible starting point for this project would be to contact local Parent Teacher Association groups and inform them of your concerns.

Resources for Further Study

American Friends' Service Committee. *The Global Factory.* A study guide; see above, p. 36, for address to order.

Brown, Robert McAfee. *Theology in a New Key.* Philadelphia: Westminster, 1978.

Gutiérrez, Gustavo. *A Theology of Liberation.* Maryknoll: Orbis, 1973; rev. ed., 1988.

Lernoux, Penny. *Cry of the People.* New York: Doubleday, 1980.

Third-World Resources. *Food, Hunger, Agribusiness.*

_____ *Human Rights: A Directory of Resources.* Both books are study guides; see above, p. 36, for address to order.

Chapter Four

Trevia, A Black Child Living in Poverty

The Imaginative Journey

My great-great grandparents came up in slavery. Big Mama sometimes tells me stories about the old days. Whatever the white folks said to do, they did. They worked sunup to sundown, never got paid anything. They lived in tiny little cabins and the white family had a big house. When they wanted to visit off the place, they had to have passes. Anyone found without a pass, the patrollers whipped. Life was hard in those old slave days.

Sometimes old folks say we've taken the shackles of slavery from our hands and feet, but we're still working to take them from our minds. Big Mama says we still carry the burden of our past on our backs.

Mama and Papa fought. I don't know why. Papa worked in the hospital. He was an orderly, and some of the doctors said he could read x-rays better than they could. After integration, he sent my oldest sister Roberta to the white school. The police in Battleborough were bad to throw their weight around when a black man challenged white rules. They started to follow Papa everywhere. He got nervous and took to drinking. The hospital fired him, and one night the police picked him up drunk and beat him so badly that he died. Mama had fought with him all those years, but she couldn't seem to get over his death. She left me with my grandmama and took Roberta and Arletta up North to Chicago.

I love Big Mama. She whips me if I don't mind, but she loves me and fights for me if anyone tries to make me feel ashamed of myself. Big Mama works for the Pryors, a white family. They give her their hand-me-down clothes and left-over food. They pay her twenty-five dollars a day, and she works for them three days a week. She cooks and cleans and irons, and takes care of the children when Mrs. Pryor goes out to shop or play bridge.

Rent is two hundred dollars a month. Then we pay utilities and bus fare, and I have to have clothes for school. Big Mama says education is the path to a better future.

I don't know how we would buy food without food stamps.

Some children in school have it worse than I do. Some of them live in three-room houses with seven or eight in the family. It's never quiet to read or do their homework.

Big Mama says it used to be a little easier to get by. Now the government gives less help and makes it harder to get food stamps. That's why we barely make it every month. We can't afford to get sick.

Big Mama gives me the best food and keeps the slim pickings for herself. She always eats the wings and back of a chicken. Last winter she had the flu for several weeks, and we had to borrow money from the Pryors. To pay it back we had to cut out sugar and other things for several months.

One day when I was walking to school, a car of white teenagers came by fast and drove so close to me that I had to jump into the ditch. They laughed. Dust got all over my school clothes. It seems like sometimes just to have a black face invites trouble.

But Big Mama says God made me just the way I am because God likes me just that way. She says I should never be ashamed of who I am, and people who judge other people by the color of their skin are ignorant. They don't know any better.

What I like best about Big Mama is, she knows when to laugh and when to cry and when to stand up and show folks what she's made of.

Some day I want to be a ballet dancer. I watched a ballet on television and it was beautiful. I like to imagine myself sweeping across the stage, moving through the air like I am about to fly. Nancy and Ansley Pryor take ballet lessons. We can't afford them.

At nights when Big Mama turns out the kitchen lights I dance there in secret.

Scriptural Reflections

The Word of God

Then little children were being brought to him in order that he might lay his hands on them and pray. The disciples spoke sternly to those who brought them; but Jesus said, "Let the little children come to me, and do not stop them; for it is to such as these that the kingdom of heaven belongs." And he laid his hands on them and went on his way (Matthew 19:13-15).

Prayer Response

Lord, your reign belongs to children. You call us to believe, as children do, in the future you proclaim—in a world in which all have enough to eat, in which the meek thrive and the last are first.

In our nation today, a shocking percentage of children is poor; this number has grown dramatically in recent years. Many of these poor children have inherited a history of racial discrimination and systematic oppression.

Help us to consider the future we prepare for these children—and for our nation—when we stand by passive as they grow up in poverty. They will be handicapped by lack of education; they will grow up dulled by despair as they see no exit from the cycle of poverty.

Help us to see that these are *our* children. What happens to them is *our* responsibility. We confess our sinfulness in allowing so many children to live in poverty, in living as if we have no obligation to them.

We commit ourselves to your will that these children be set free from poverty. Help us to love them as you love them.

The Word of God

At that time the disciples came to Jesus and asked, "Who is the greatest in the kingdom of heaven?" And he called a child, whom he put among them, and said, "Truly I tell you, unless you change and become like children, you will never enter the kingdom of heaven. Whoever becomes humble like this child is the greatest in the kingdom of heaven. Whoever welcomes one such child in my name welcomes me. If any of you put a stumbling block before one of these little ones who believe in me, it would be better for you if a great millstone were fastened around your neck and you were drowned in the depth of the sea. Woe to the world because of stumbling blocks! Occasions for stumbling are bound to come, but woe to the one by whom the stumbling block comes! (Matthew 18:1-7).

Prayer Response

Alas to the one who causes the little ones to stumble! Your words strike our hearts, Lord.

We worry about the increased crime rates in our cities, about acts of senseless violence and drug abuse. But we spend too little time worrying about the roots of these problems. Forgive us that we selfishly fail to think of homes broken by the strains of poverty, of living conditions that crush the human spirit, of educations that do not nurture the precious gifts of each individual, of the despair that grows as one foresees a future as bleak as the present.

These are the roots from which the crime and drug abuse of our cities grow. We have the power to deal with these roots. We do not do so, and we are painfully aware that your word addresses *us*: woe to us if we place stumbling blocks before the children of our world.

Prayers from the Religions of the World

One day we will have to stand before the God of history and we will talk in terms of things we've done. Yes, we will be able to say we built gargantuan bridges to span the seas, we built gigantic buildings to kiss the skies. Yes, we made our submarines to penetrate oceanic depths. We brought into being many other things with our scientific and technological power.

Martin Luther King, Jr.

It seems that I can hear the God of history saying, "That was not enough! But I was hungry and ye fed me not. I was naked and ye clothed me not. I was devoid of a decent sanitary house to live in, and ye provided no shelter for me. And consequently, you cannot enter the kingdom of greatness. If ye do it unto the least of these, my brethren, ye do it unto me." That's the question facing America today.[25]

*   *   *

James Weldon Johnson, the African-American National Anthem

Lord, so speaks your prophet Martin.
You do not judge as we judge.
We pride ourselves on our ability to span the seas
And plumb the ocean depths,
But many little ones in our midst hunger and thirst and go un-
clothed.

Fill us with your Spirit of discernment:
Help us to see what *needs* to be done.
Fill us with your Spirit of fortitude:
Enable us to struggle for justice in an unjust world.

*   *   *

Lift every voice and sing
Till earth and heaven ring,
Ring with the harmonies of Liberty;
Let our rejoicing rise
High as the listening skies,

---

25. "Remaining Awake through a Great Revolution," in *A Testament of Hope: The Essential Writings of Martin Luther King, Jr.,* ed. James M. Washington (New York: Harper & Row, 1986), 275.

Let it resound loud as the rolling sea.
Sing a song full of the faith that the dark past has
    taught us,
Sing a song full of the hope that the present has
    brought us.
Facing the rising sun of our new day begun,
Let us march on till victory is won.

Stony the road we trod,
Bitter the chastening rod,
Felt in the days when hope unborn had died;
Yet with a steady beat,
Have not our weary feet
Come to the place for which our fathers sighed?
We have come over a way that with tears has been
    watered,
We have come, treading our path through the blood of
    the slaughtered,
Out from the gloomy past,
Till now we stand at last
Where the white gleam of our bright star is cast.

God of our weary years,
God of our silent tears,
Thou who has brought us thus far on the way;
Thou who has by Thy might
Led us into the light,
Keep us forever in the path, we pray.
Lest our feet stray from the places, our God, where we
    met Thee,
Lest, our hearts drunk with the wine of the world, we
    forget Thee;

Shadowed beneath Thy hand,
May we forever stand.
True to our God,
True to our native land.[26]

*   *   *

Anonymous

O Lord, remember not only the men and women of good will,
but also those of ill will. But do not remember all the suffering
they have inflicted on us; remember the fruits we have bought,
thanks to this suffering—our comradeship, our loyalty, our humility, our courage, our generosity, the greatness of heart which has
grown out of all this, and when they come to judgement let all the
fruits which we have borne be their forgiveness.[27]

*   *   *

George Appleton

The sins of the world,
such dreadful sins.
not just the personal sins
but the solidarity of sin
greater than the total
of individual sins
nuclear evil in endless fission
O Lamb of God

The sin of racial pride
that sees not the faith

26.   Langston Hughes and Anna Bontemp's, ed., *Poetry of the American Negro,
1746-1970* (NY: Doubleday, 1970).
27.   Prayer written by an unknown prisoner in Ravensbrück concentration camp
and left beside the body of a dead Jewish child. See *Oxford Book of Prayer*, 112.

that all men are divinely made
nor the riches of pigment
in portrait faces,
the same psychology
and religious search,
that each is the sibling
for whom Christ died.

The burgeoning greed
that never heeds the needs of others
involved in a merciless system.
looking only at profit and dividend,
the last of possessions
that cannot accompany us
at our last migration:
Take away these sins,
O Lamb of God.[28]

*   *   *

James Baldwin

Everything now, we must assume, is in our hands; we have no
right to assume otherwise. If we—and now I mean the relatively
conscious whites and the relatively conscious blacks, who must,
like lovers, insist on, or create, the consciousness of the others—do
not falter in our duty now, we may be able, handful that we are, to
end the racial nightmare, and achieve our country, and change the
history of the world. If we do not now dare everything, the fulfillment of that prophecy, recreated from the Bible in song by a slave,
is upon us: *God gave Noah the rainbow sign, No more water, the fire
next time!*[29]

---

28. George Appleton, *The Word Is the Seed* (London: SPCK, 1976), 82-4.
29. *The Fire Next Time* (New York: Dell, 1962), 141.

Lord, save us from the fire next time!
Give us vision and courage
To unravel the nets of injustice
We have woven for centuries,
To reweave the fabric of our societies
So that all live together in harmony,
In peace and justice.

Actions on Behalf of Justice for Poor Minority Children

February is Black History Month in the United States. Schools, parishes, and churches around the country commemorate the month with art exhibits, poetry readings, plays, lectures, and other activities. You could take part in this celebration by helping to organize Black History Month projects in your church or school.

Possible projects would be having children compose collages about African-American life and history, inviting speakers, reading and discussing texts, or inviting a black church choir to give a performance of spirituals. In the celebrations, try to emphasize that the quest for racial justice needs to stay alive in an America that has turned its back on this quest in the past several decades.

*   *   *

Social analysts note that poverty is never accidental: social forces create poverty and keep some groups poor while others thrive. The United States is now the first industrialized nation in the world in which children are the poorest age group.

You can form a study group to examine why children are poor today. Possible resources include the Congressional Research Service's *Children in Poverty*; Murray, *Losing Ground*; and Harrington, *New American Poverty*.

* * *

Many activists, ministers, and political commentators think that federal policies over the past two decades have virtually ended the civil rights movement. Supreme Court decisions have limited affirmative action programs, and welfare cutbacks and cuts in aid to university students have made it less likely that impoverished black Americans can rise out of their poverty. You might accept the challenge of activists to urge your congressional representatives to support the civil rights movement and to work to eradicate poverty among American children.

* * *

Lobbying is a very effective means of garnering political support for the goals of one's cause. You may decide to support lobbies to increase welfare benefits for single mothers, to increase the minimum wage, to pass stricter legislation requiring employers to provide benefits, to raise the standards of public schools, particularly in deprived areas, and to pass legislation requiring landlords to maintain decent housing. Groups such as the Center of Concern (see *Actions* list for Journey I) and Bread for the World (see *Actions* list for Journey III) contribute to such lobbying efforts.

* * *

In most Western, industrialized countries, the tax system assures that those who benefit the most from the economic system in turn contribute proportionately more to that system through the taxes they pay. Many political scientists note that the American tax system tends to function differently than this: it benefits the wealthy and burdens the poor.

You may wish to inform youself about this issue. A good beginning resource is the National Conference of Catholic Bishops' *Economic Justice for All*, especially chapter 3B. See also Pechman, *Who Paid Taxes?*

* * *

Most communities have programs or clinics providing medical services for poor children or nutritional education programs for mothers of poor children. You may consider volunteering your services to such a program or clinic. A good way to inquire about such programs might be to telephone government or other social services agencies in your community.

*　　　*　　　*

In most areas of the country there is a growing need for adequate daycare for children of working mothers. In some areas, those concerned about this need have formed associations to study the availability of daycare in the community, and standards of existing daycare centers. If there is such an association in your community, you might join it. If there is no such group, you may wish to form one.

*　　　*　　　*

Racism exists in every corner of our land, in both the attitudes of our people and the structures of our society. You may wish to form a church or parish study group to examine this social disease and to discuss ways to heal it.

A very good resource for such a study group is *Racism: America's Original Sin,* available from the Sojourners Resource Center, Box 29272, Washington, DC 20017.

Resources for Further Study

Congressional Research Service. *Children in Poverty.* Washington, DC, May 22, 1985.

Harrington, Michael. *The New American Poverty.* New York: Holt, Rinehart and Winston, 1984.

Murray, Charles. *Losing Ground: American Social Policy 1950-1980.* New York: Basic Books, 1984.

National Conference of Catholic Bishops. *Economic Justice for All.* Washington, DC: U.S. Catholic Conference, 1986.

Pechman, Joseph. *Who Paid Taxes, 1965-85?* Washington, DC: The Brookings Institution, 1985.

Sojourners Resource Center. *America's Original Sin: A Study Guide on White Racism.* A study guide; see above, p. 50, for address to order.

Chapter Five

The Seiberts, A Dispossessed Farm Family

The Imaginative Journey

This is good land.

When our great grandparents came to it, they were amazed at its length and breadth, its riches there for the taking if they were willing to work. They worked hard.

There were trees to clear, stones to pick out of the fields, gardens to make. They *built* the land. They believed it was wrong to take from the earth and give nothing back. Year by year, generation after generation, we have carefully put back into our land what the crops have taken from it. Grandpa used to say that the Bible verses about good stewardship are not just good theology: they're good farm sense.

Great Grandfather Adam Seibert wrote some letters back to the old country. They speak of this new land as a garden of Eden, a place where those who work hard have an assured place on the land, a secure old age, a dream of a better life for their children and their children's children. Grandfather Adam's letters give thanks to the God who provides so lavishly, whose love is so evident in the good things of the earth.

The first year Grandfather Adam and Grandmother Johanna settled this land, they cleared as much of it as they could and then planted an orchard. You have never seen anything so beautiful as that orchard. In spring it's like a song sung by the earth itself—the delicate colors of the blossoms, the birds sheltering in the new leaves. In summer the beauty changes: ripening fruit that hangs heavy and inviting on the trees. Even in winter the trees have a peculiar loveliness; their bare branches stand out against the winter sky as a promise that the year will eventually renew itself, that nothing wicked will finally triumph over the goodness of the creator God.

Tomorrow that orchard will be cut down.

At the beginning of the year, we had to sell out. We had intended for our family to live always on this land.

It is good land, and we had made it better. But in the past few years, life on the farm has gotten harder and harder. Seiberts' is a family farm, a medium-sized farm. We *wanted* to be a family farm. Grandfather had the opportunity to buy another half section at a very good price, and he refused to do so. "I have good land, enough for a good life and to give my children a good life," he said. Our belief has always been that a family cannot care for too much land the way it should be cared for.

But in recent years the federal government has told us to get bigger or get out. All the government talk about saving the family farm has a hollow sound for us, because the government policies always favor large landholders. We have seen more and more farms around us sold for tax shelters to professional people in the cities, or to large corporations who want to manage them as profitable "land-factories." These were farms that had always supported families of good neighbors.

On Sunday afternoons our family outing is to drive around the area and look at the neighboring farms. More and more we see land neglected and exploited. When a farm is farmed by people who don't own or live on it, it quickly runs down. When a farm is farmed only to make money, the soil is depleted. These factory farmers and absentee owners do not seem to understand that you have to replenish the loam and fertility of the soil as you take from it. Abused land becomes so thin that it blows and washes away. It hurts to see good, well-managed farms vanishing before our eyes.

The land is a non-renewable resource. What will happen when we have squandered all of it?

Getting bigger means buying new, more expensive machinery. Buying new machinery means going deeper into debt. In addition to buying machinery, we had to use more chemical fertilizer, pesticides and herbicides. We worried about the long-term effects on the land.

After a few years of using heavy chemicals, we began to see that many of the birds that had once visited the farm in spring and summer were not returning. By destroying the "pests" on which they fed, we were upsetting an ecological cycle that encouraged them to come. We had always had some of the best water in the country. Tests began to show seepage of chemicals into our well. But if the pressure to produce in order to keep your head above water is so intense, what can you do?

Eventually, we had to face our neighbors' fate. After several years of warning as our debt accumulated, the bank foreclosed on us. We saw this coming. We worked as hard as we could—*all* of us in the family worked—but we could not avoid the inevitable.

Now a large corporation with thousands of acres in the state will run our farm as a food factory. We know from experience that that corporation will not have our scruples about using chemical fertilizers and herbicides or pesticides. The farm will be "managed" by hired managers who do not live on it.

The old Seibert place will be torn down. This house has seen several generations of our family be born and die. To bring in more income, the corporation is going to cut down the orchard and use that piece of land for a mobile home park. Some of our former neighbors have told us they plan to buy mobile homes and live there. Their houses are gone, too. Some of them now work as hired hands on the new corporation farms in the area.

We plan to move into the city. We have always been resourceful, and we can make our way. But we leave our land with heavy hearts.

What hurts most of all is that we did what our country tells good citizens to do: we worked hard, contributed to the community and its schools and churches, and kept the law. But our country's promise that those who work hard and live uprightly will prosper failed us. What went wrong?

Our children wanted to farm.

It seems somehow that a promise had been made to them, too. And it is not being kept.

Scriptural Reflections

The Word of God

See, I have set before you today life and prosperity, death and adversity. If you obey the commandments of the Lord your God that I am commanding you today, by loving the Lord your God, walking in his ways, and observing his commandments, decrees, and ordinances, then you shall live and become numerous, and the Lord your God will bless you in the land that you are entering to possess. But if your heart turns away and you do not hear, but are led astray to bow down to other gods and serve them, I declare to you today that you shall perish; you shall not live long in the land that you are crossing the Jordan to enter and possess. I call heaven and earth to witness against you today that I have set before you life and death, blessings and hope. Choose life so that you and your descendants may live, loving the Lord your God, obeying him, and holding fast to him; for that means life to you and length of days, so that you may live in the land the Lord swore to give to your ancestors, to Abraham, to Isaac, and to Jacob (Deuteronomy 30: 15-20).

Prayer Response

You brought our foreparents into a very good land, a land flowing with milk and honey. We sing of amber fields of grain and purple mountains' majesty. We celebrate the goodness of this land of promise and great hope.

But even as we rejoice and give thanks, we recall your challenge to us: *Choose life!* You have made us stewards of this fertile land of breathtaking beauty. And now we must ask ourselves if we have indeed chosen life, if we have used the land as you desire.

We see vast farmlands owned by the few, who do not cherish the land itself and who wish to use it for material gain. We see our streams fouled and our mountainsides gashed and left as open wounds, all because of the heedless quest for easy money. We breathe air that carries noxious fumes. We eat food that may slowly poison us.

We have not chosen life.

The good earth does not have to turn against us. It does so only when we turn against it, and you its Maker.

Call us back to you, Lord, to careful stewardship, to life itself. Give us a burning desire to oppose the greed that exploits and destroys, and that does not count the cost of exploitation and destruction. Help us to recall the dream of our foremothers and forefathers, a dream of the good life for all in this good land to which you have brought us.

The Word of God

Happy is everyone who fears the Lord,
   who walks in his ways.
You shall eat the fruit of the
   labor of your hands;
you shall be happy, and it
   shall go well with you

Your wife will be like a fruitful vine
   within your house;
your children will be like olive shoots
   around your table.
Thus shall the one be blessed
   who fear the Lord.

The Lord bless you from Zion.
   May you see the prosperity of Jerusalem
all the days of your life.
May you see your children's children.
   Peace be upon Israel! (Psalm 128).

Prayer Response

Lord, we bless you for the work you set before us. In tilling the earth and making it bear fruit, in shaping the gifts of the earth to enrich our lives, we share in your creative love. You call us to something astonishing—to share with you in creating the world.

Make us worthy of the task. Make us aware of the dignity of labor. Help us to build a world in which all shall be free to labor with dignity and hope, in which the abundant gifts of all shall be appreciated.

The Word of God

Is not this the fast that I choose, to loose the bonds of injustice, to undo the thongs of the yoke, to let the oppressed go free, and to break every yoke? Is it not to share your bread with the hungry, and bring the homeless poor into your house; when you see the naked, to cover them, and not to hide yourself from your own kin? Then you light shall break forth like the dawn, and your healing shall spring up quickly; your vindicator shall go before you, the glory of the Lord shall be your rear guard. Then you shall call, and the Lord will answer; you shall cry for help, and he will say, "Here I am." If you remove the yoke from among you, the pointing of the finger, the speaking of evil, if you offer your food to the hungry and satisfy the needs of the afflicted, then your light shall rise in the darkness and your gloom be like the noonday. The Lord will guide you continually, and satisfy your needs in parched places, and make your bones strong; and you shall be like a watered garden, like a spring of water, whose waters never fail. Your ancient ruins shall be rebuilt; you shall raise up the foundations of many generations; you shall be called the repairer of the breach, the restorer of streets to live in (Isaiah 58:6-12).

Prayer Response

Lord, you call us to make justice flourish in our land. To do so is to worship you. You tell us that when we do justice, the land itself will bless us with its good gifts.

We commit ourselves to the struggle for justice. We do so with the dispossessed farm families of our land. We pledge ourselves to create a more just economy, one which does not penalize the small farmer and favor the large farmer, one which does not place a crushing economic burden on the backs of families who labor daily and do not reap the reward of their labor. We pledge ourselves to solidarity with farm families, because we know that their labor is necessary—it feeds us.

The Word of God

And he said to them, "Take care! Be on your guard against all kinds of greed; for one's life does not consist in the abundance of possessions." Then he told them a parable: "The land of a rich man produced abundantly. And he thought to himself, 'What should I do, for I have no place to store my crops?' Then he said, 'I will do this: I will pull down my barns and build larger ones, and there I will store all my grain and my goods. *And I will say to my soul, 'Soul, you have ample goods laid up for many years; relax, eat, drink, be merry.' But God said to him, 'You fool! This very night your life is being demanded of you. And the things you have prepared, whose will they be?' So it is with those who store up treasures for themselves but are not rich toward God"* (Luke 12:13-21).

Prayer Response

Lord, we are weary. We are weary of the search for endless wealth. Our society tells us that just one more thing—a bigger house, a more glamorous car—will satisfy our inner hunger. But when we have that thing, our hunger remains. We drink from cups with holes in their bottoms, rather than from the fountain of life itself, You.

We are weary of the rationalizations the powerful of the world use to justify their greed: the pretense that their hoarding of the goods of the world is for the benefit of us all rather than for their benefit; the argument that unthinking exploitation of the land is "progress," or "daring entrepreneurship."

We tire of hearing callous selfishness masked as economic virtue. We hear the words of your parable against greed. Your words expose as lies many of the justifications of our own economic system.

We commit ourselves to build an economy in which a few will not be allowed to monopolize the good things of the earth, while the many are in want.

Prayers from the Religions of the World

Sioux Indian Prayer

Ho! Great Spirit, Grandfather, you have made everything and are in everything. You sustain everything, guide everything, provide everything and protect everything because everything belongs to you. I am weak, poor and lowly, nevertheless help me to care in appreciation and gratitude to you and for everything. I love the stars, the sun and the moon and I thank you for our beautiful mother the earth whose many breasts nourish the fish, the fowls and the animals too. May I never deceive mother earth, may I never deceive other people, may I never deceive myself, and above all may I never deceive you (Bishop Vine Deloria).[30]

*   *   *

Shaker Hymn

'Tis the gift to be simple, 'tis the gift to be free,
'Tis the gift to come down where we ought to be.
And when we find ourselves in the place just right,
'Twill be in the valley of love and delight.

When true simplicity is gain'd,
To bow and to bend we shan't be asham'd,
To turn, turn will be our delight
'Till by turning, turning we come round right.

*   *   *

Ernst Block

The earth has room for everyone, or it would have, if it were run by the power of satisfying people's needs instead of by satisfying the needs of power.[31]

*   *   *

Lord, you do not create wantonly.
All that you call to being has a place in your plan.
Forgive us that we make so many among us marginal,
Because we are unwilling to relinquish our stranglehold
On what we call our own.

---

30. *Oxford Book of Prayer*, 352.
31. *The Principle of Hope*, Neville Plaice, Stephen Plaice, and Paul Knight (Cambridge, MA: 1986), 2.469.

Help us to recall that what we hold in excess of our need
Belongs to those who need it,
Because it belongs first and foremost to you,
The giver of all good gifts.

*   *   *

Lozi prayer from Nambia

O Nyambe [God], you are the creator of all. Today we your creatures prostrate ourselves before you in supplication. We have no strength. You who have created us have all power. We bring you our seed and all our implements, that you may bless them and bless us also that we may make good use of them by the power which comes from you, our creator.[32]

*   *   *

W.E.B. DuBois

Grant us, O God, the vision and the will to be found on the right side in the great battle for bread, which rages round us, in strike and turmoil and litigation. Let us remember that here as so often elsewhere no impossible wisdom is asked of men [and women], only Thine ancient sacrifice—to do justly and love mercy and walk humbly—to refuse to use, of the world's goods, more than we earn, to be generous with those that earn but little and to avoid the vulgarity that flaunts wealth and clothes and ribbons in the face of poverty. These things are the sins that lie beneath our labor wars, and from such sins defend us, O Lord. Amen.

Actions on Behalf of Justice for Farmers

In a number of communities, consumer groups and study groups have formed to examine the marketing and distribution policies of food companies in their areas. Questions asked by such groups include these: are locally grown products available in local

---

32.   John S. Mbiti, ed., *The Prayers of African Religion* (London: SPCK, 1975), 66.

stores? What happens to local products, if they do not in fact appear in local food stores? What criteria are used in food pricing?

Do local stores and food companies protect consumer interests by practicing fair labeling and by scrutinizing the quality of products sold? How do buying and pricing policies affect local farmers? Do local food companies promote ecological consciousness in their packaging and in their buying policies; do they offer organically grown local produce? You may wish to form a consumer group to ask such questions in your community.

* * *

If large corporate-owned food stores in a community do not make it a priority to buy directly from local farmers, to promote ecological awareness, or to offer chemical-free produce, groups in such communities sometimes form co-op food stores.

If your community does not have such a co-op, you may decide to help organize one. For advice, you might ask other such ventures in nearby areas how they started and how they operate. If a co-op does exist in your community, you may wish to become active in it.

* * *

In recent years many researchers have noted that North American consumption habits have a deleterious effect on the health of North Americans themselves, on the ecosystem of the planet, and on the food supply of third-world countries. Among the findings of researchers is that Americans eat far more meat than necessary to sustain a healthy existence; American consumption of meat, and particularly of beef, is growing. To raise cattle requires that a great deal of grain (which humans can consume) be converted to animal protein; from the standpoint of its effect on world food supplies, this is a wasteful process, one that sometimes causes food products of third-world countries to be sold to cattle raisers in the first world.

In some communities, classes and study groups have been organized to teach people to modify their conspicuous consumption by eating lower on the food chain. If you decide to start or participate in such a project, indispensable resources include Lappé, *Diet for a Small Planet* and *Food First*.

*　　　　*　　　　*

A sign of hope in some cities is gardens planted by citizens on unused, public city land. This sign of hope demonstrates for all to see that our cities can provide green spaces if we choose for them to do so, and that people can work together to build a healthier lifestyle.

Perhaps you can discover whether it is possible for your city to make unused public lands available for those who wish to grow gardens. One possible starting point for such an inquiry would be to contact your city councilperson for information.

*　　　　*　　　　*

As the preceding imaginative journey suggests, the crisis in which American family farmers today find themselves is rooted in federal agricultural policies. Activists recommend writing your congresspersons to ask about about their view regarding the agricultural policies of the government.

Ask your representatives what they are doing to reverse the trend of farm foreclosures and the conversion of American agriculture into a big-business, for-profit industry. Consult ratings that grade the performance of your congressional members in the area of concern for family farmers, and publicize your findings. An informative resource for information on the family farm is Strange, *Family Farming*.

*　　　　*　　　　*

Those who promote the interests of family farmers must compete against powerful lobbies organized by large corporations. Those corporations that produce and package our food also often produce industrial products or weapons. The large holdings and wealth of such corporations give them even more clout in determining federal agricultural policies. You may wish to participate in lobbying efforts to change the federal policy of rewarding large farmers and penalizing small ones.

Two organizations concerned with such issues are the Institute for Food and Development Policy, 145 Ninth Street, San Francisco, CA 94103; and the National Catholic Rural Life Conference, which publishes a newsletter entitled *Common Ground*, providing information about federal legislation affecting agriculture. NCRLC's address is 4625 Beaver Ave., Des Moines, IA 50310-2199; (515) 270-2634.

*   *   *

Social activists urge us to boycott the products of those large corporations that blatantly exploit the land and damage the environment. You can decide to participate in such boycotts.

An organization that provides information on these matters is the Council on Economic Priorities; a reference to this group appears in Journey II. A helpful resource published by this group is Will, et al., *Shopping for a Better World*.

*   *   *

In many schools, churches, and parishes, farm-awareness programs raise the consciousness of the local community about issues important to farmers. You may choose to organize such a program for your church or school. Seek to make participants aware of the country's dependence on farmers and of the present crisis in agriculture. You could sponsor an exhibit of local farm products or of posters depicting the food-production chain of your area.

*   *   *

An important area of study for a church or parish study group is ecology. Many contemporary scholars of religion note that there are discernible links between how a religious tradition views the natural world, and whether it exploits or cherishes the environment.

Perhaps you can form a study group to examine this topic. Your group ought to look at the various religions of the world for resources to enable people to develop a reverent and respectful attitude to the ecosystem. A good beginning guide is McDaniel, *Earth, Sky, Gods, and Mortals*.

Resources for Further Study

Lappé, Frances Moore. *Diet for a Small Planet*. Rev. ed. New York: Random House, 1975.

_____ *Food First: Beyond the Myth of Scarcity*. Boston: Houghton, Mifflin, 1977.

McDaniel, Jay. *Earth, Sky, Gods, and Mortals*. Mystic, CT: Twenty-Third, 1990.

Strange, Marty. *Family Farming: A New Economic Vision*. San Francisco: Food First, 1989.

Will, Rosalyn, et al., *Shopping for a Better World*. New York: Council on Economic Priorities, 1989.

Chapter Six

Michael, An AIDS Patient

The Imaginative Journey

Dear David,

I need to talk to you.

Growing up, we never really talked about sex. In fact, I never let myself think about what I felt was true: that I was gay. The words were so ugly—faggot, queer, fruit, fairy. When I heard them, I cringed inside. I felt they applied to me, but denied it at the same time.

Remember those wonderful teen years? Dances, proms, goofing off with the guys? I never told you, but they were a time of terrible inner struggle for me. I suppose this is true for many people. But added to the normal confusion about growing adult identity and sexual maturity, I lived in frightening confusion about whether my very instincts were warped.

Did you ever try to control an instinct? It's not easy, even when you know that acting on it might harm someone else. In my case, the instinct seemed to be part of what religion and society call normal and good. Love opens one up, makes one feel a sense of self-worth and self-transcendence. But it was love itself that seemed to be the problem for me.

Of course I never thought about these issues frankly when you and I were teenagers. I simply tried to keep an inner lid on my thoughts. They were frightening. I attempted to do what was expected. I dated and went to dances and experimented timidly with sex with girls. But when I did so, it was as if some other person inhabited my body. The real me was elsewhere, distant from what I was doing.

I once tried to talk about some of this with Father Ken. Remember him? Our high school chaplain? He was sympathetic. He talked about God's love, and the need to love and accept ourselves. But he also told me that I was just going through a phase and would outgrow it in time. He encouraged me to emulate Jesus and seek purity. After that, I simply stopped trying to deal with my hidden thoughts in any way. I decided the church was right, after all: it *is* best to be chaste. I closed myself, hardened myself, against what I called temptations of the flesh.

Then in college something happened. It was like a dam bursting. Another guy showed an interest in me, and I felt attracted, keenly so. I told myself that this was a friendship of extraordinary beauty and intensity, but I knew deep inside that my feelings were growing increasingly erotic. The relationship itself seemed so good for me. I felt as if before I had been going through every day with hidden armor that protected me by cutting me off from life, hope, joy. Now I felt loved, and life itself seemed good, full of possibility. My grades soared. I became the life of the party.

Then one night after a party, he invited me to his apartment. We talked, drank wine, and then it happened—sex. The next day I went to the park and walked and tried to think. I *was* what all those ugly names said, a social outcast, a rebel against God. I was torn. What had happened seemed good and liberating, but I felt that my very delight condemned me.

I decided to shut myself off from the occasion of sin. I went to Mass daily and prayed more fervently. I felt such inner anguish that at times I wondered if I would simply go crazy. I found it difficult to know what people meant when they talked about God as love.

After several months of this, I came home for the summer vacation. You probably remember that summer, my first summer home from college? The whole summer, I was as out of sorts as a bear just waking from its winter sleep. Mom sensed I was troubled and attempted to talk, but I held back. Since she often asked coyly about girlfriends and talked about how happy she would be to see me married and settled, I did not think I could open up.

Then I "fell" again. This time it was more deliberate. I went to a shopping center where I had noticed men hanging around the restrooms. Though I was nervous and unsure, I met a man who took me home. If I told you his name, you'd flip. Mr. X was middle-aged, a pillar of the community, in fact. His wife was away for the weekend.

After this, I decided that, since I apparently could not live according to the moral dictates of Christianity, I must simply reject the church altogether. I stopped going to Mass. I stopped praying. I returned to college, got an apartment, and began to live a promiscuous life. It was a life of danger, an unsatisfying life. I once brought home someone who assaulted me and robbed me. I called the police and had them take me to an emergency room; when they arrived at the apartment, they laughed and made brutal comments about my sexual life.

I now wonder if I was promiscuous *because* I felt worthless and unwanted, a social pariah. Was I deliberately self-destructive? To use the jargon of the sociology textbooks, was I internalizing against myself the violence that society directs to those defined as sexually aberrant?

Six months ago I discovered that I tested positive for the human immunodeficiency virus. You'll probably know it as the AIDS virus. The disease is slowly progressing, and I now have symptoms that indicate I may become much sicker in a few years.

It may sound strange for me to say so, Dave, but this has been a good time in my life. I don't by any means want to say that sickness and suffering are good. They're not; they are destructive forces that should always be confronted and eradicated when it is possible to do so.

What has been good is that the illness has forced me to take a long look at myself. I like what I find. I am not the monster I thought myself. I am slowly healing inside, and part of the healing is that I am discovering God is for me and not against me.

Recently I had the good fortune to meet a priest who ministers to AIDS patients, and we talk almost daily. He has helped me to see that the face of the church I encountered and rejected is just that—a face, not the church itself. The church follows in the footsteps of Jesus who always met disease and pain with healing compassion. I now realize that, though the church is called to do as Jesus did, its actual practice often fails to conform to the example of Jesus. Remember how we used to give hell to Mr. D'Anna, our high school religion teacher, about "holy wars"?   Well, the church's treatment of sexual outcasts hasn't been much different than those holy wars—a violation of everything the gospel calls the church to believe and do.

I have begun to pray again, to be good to myself by eating well, exercising, and forming healthy bonds with others. I never knew that life could be so good.

I'm writing this because I want you to know what's going on with me, David.

Love,
Michael

P.S. We're brothers. We should share our lives and struggles.

Scriptural Reflections

The Word of God

Thus says the Lord: Maintain justice, and do what is right, for soon my salvation will come, and my deliverance be revealed. Happy is the mortal who does this, the one who holds it fast, who keeps the sabbath, not profaning it, and refrains from doing any evil. Do not let the foreigner joined to the Lord say, "The Lord will surely separate me from his people"; and do not let the eunuch say, "I am just a dry tree." For thus says the Lord: To the eunuchs who keep my sabbaths, who choose the things that please me and hold fast my covenant, I will give, in my house and within my walls, a monument and a name better than sons and daughters; I will give them an everlasting name that shall not be cut off . . . their burnt offerings and their sacrifices will be accepted on my altar; for my house shall be called a house or prayer for all peoples. Thus says the Lord God, who gathers the outcasts of Israel, I will gather others to them besides those already gathered (Isaiah 56:1-5, 7-8).

Prayer Response

Lord, we praise you for your magnificent grace, your love that reaches out to all, and particularly the outcast. You call all to your house of prayer; there you give the eunuch a place and a name.

As we hear your saving words and see the breadth of your compassion, we know that we fall short. We have not loved as you have loved. We have excluded and judged. We have not made all welcome in your house.

Forgive us. We commit ourselves to compassionate solidarity with all social outcasts, and particularly to our brothers and sisters who are sick with AIDS.

The Word of God

That evening, at sundown, they brought to him all who were sick or possessed with demons. And the whole city was gathered around the door. And he cured many who were sick with various diseases, and cast out many demons; and he would not permit the demons to speak, because they knew him (Mark 1:32-33).

Prayer Response

Lord Jesus, you healed. The gospels show you healing all who came to you sick. You never judged. You never told the sick to be patient with their sickness because God willed them to be ill. You refused to preach that God sends disease as a punishment for sin.

We who walk in your way and call ourselves your followers are called to heal as you healed. Strengthen us to fight against any tendency to stigmatize those who are ill. Help us to resist the compulsion to link disease with God's will. Give us eyes to see you suffering in our sick brothers and sisters.

The Word of God

Then Levi gave a great banquet for him in his house; and there was a large crowd of tax collectors and others sitting at the table with them. The Pharisees and their scribes were complaining to his disciples, saying, "Why do you eat and drink with tax collectors and sinners?" Jesus answered, "Those who are well have no need of a physician, but those who are sick; I have come to call not the righteous but sinners to repentance (Luke 5:29-32).

Prayer Response

Lord, your ministry was to the outcast. You broke social taboos. You made solidarity with those your society regarded as public sinners beyond the pale of righteousness. You did this to remind us that we all stand before God as sinners. We all are the sick you came to heal.

Heal us above all of the disease of self-righteousness, of the grave illness of thinking that we do not stand in need of your mercy. As you heal us, send us out to do as you did: to make solidarity with those our society casts out.

You invited yourself to the house of Zacchaeus the tax-collector when he considered himself unworthy to meet you. Help us to walk where you have walked before us.

The Word of God

He had no form or majesty that we should look at him, nothing in his appearance that we should desire him. He was despised and rejected by others; a man of suffering and acquainted with infirmity; and as one from whom others hide their faces he was despised, and we held him of no account. Surely he has borne our infirmities and carried our diseases; yet we accounted him stricken, struck down by God, and afflicted. But he was wounded for our transgressions, crushed for our iniquities, upon him was the punishment that made us whole, and by his bruises we are healed (Isaiah 53:2-6).

Prayer Response

Lord, how wondrous is your love! You become one with us even in our humiliation and suffering. To redeem us you become the outcast, the despised and downtrodden one. We take your words to heart. Help us to see that in despising the outcast, we despise you. In loving the outcast, we love you.

Prayers from the Religions of the World

Martin Israel

Let the healing grace of your love, O Lord, so transform me that I may play my part in the transfiguration of the world from a place of suffering, death and corruption to a realm of infinite light, joy and love. Make me so obedient to your Spirit that my life may become a living prayer, and a witness to your unfailing presence.[34]

*   *   *

Ancient Hindu invocation

May all that have life be delivered from suffering! (considered by the philosopher Schopenhauer the noblest of prayers).[35]

*   *   *

George Fox

O Lord, baptize our hearts into a sense of the needs and conditions of all.[35]

*   *   *

Dinka Prayer from Sudan

God help this man that he may be well; that he may recover tomorrow, and may you want to help this man to be well, and as overcoming you overcame, overcome all these troubles. And have mercy on me, because we do not know how to pray to Murungu [God] differently from what we say now.

*   *   *

---

34. Martin Israel, *The Pain That Heals* (London: Hodder & Stoughton, 1981), p. 191.
35. Ellen Glasgow, "I Believe," in Clifton Fadiman, ed., *I Believe: The Personal Philosophies of Certain Eminent Men and Women of Our Times* (NY: Simon & Schuster, 1939), 99.

Judah Ha-Levi

Heal me, my God, and I shall be healed.
Let not your anger burn, to remove me from the earth.
My potion, my medicament, depends on you
For its weakness, or its strength, its failure or its worth.
You are the one that chooses. It is not I.
For you know what is good and what is ill.
Not on my own healing do I rely.

I look only towards your powers to heal.[36]

*   *   *

Actions on Behalf of Justice for AIDS Patients

Though AIDS is often thought to be a disease of stigmatized groups such as homosexuals and intravenous drug users, HIV infection is rising among American heterosexuals and declining among homosexuals. In some groups, statistics are grim; for example, AIDS is now the number-one killer of women between the ages of 25 and 40 in New York City.

In response to the AIDS epidemic, many communities have organized programs that provide assistance and support to those who are HIV-postive or who have AIDS. You may consider training as a volunteer for such a program. A good place to go for information might be your local social services organizations.

*   *   *

Some churches and parishes have sponsored AIDS-awareness seminars. These seminars can examine how the illness is transmitted, critique social prejudices against homosexual persons, and explore resources of the church to meet the needs of AIDS patients.

---

36. *Oxford Book of Prayer*, 134.

Since a group at risk for HIV infection is sexually active teenagers, a study group can also organize or support educational programs to teach teenagers about AIDS and sexual responsibility. For suggestions regarding resource persons and how to organize such a study group, you may contact local AIDS task forces, or priests and ministers working with AIDS patients.

*   *   *

In many communities, homosexual persons have virtually no legal protection against discrimination. A majority of gay men and lesbian women in the United States report that they have experienced either verbal or physical abuse from others. Activists emphasize that we need to work for greater protection of the rights of all persons, including homosexual persons.

You may choose to support an organization that monitors the hiring and housing policies of your community with regard to homosexuals, or the record of your city's police regarding the homosexual community. If such monitoring reveals a policy of discrimination, you may wish to publicize your findings and work for laws that protect homosexual people from discrimination.

Resource groups for those who choose such an activity include New Ways Ministry, 4012-29th Street, Mt. Rainier, MD 20712 (a Catholic group); and Affirmation, P.O. Box 23636, Washington, DC 20026 (a United Methodist group).

*   *   *

AIDS activist groups have charged that the federal government's response to the AIDS crisis has been unnecessarily hesitant. They urge that we write our congresspersons to encourage them to support more funding for AIDS research, and to make response to the AIDS crisis a top medical priority of the nation.

*   *   *

Quite a few churches and parishes have sponsored prayer vigils or healing services for AIDS patients and those who work with them. If your church has not sponsored such a vigil or service, you may consider doing so. A good starting point would be to contact your pastor for information and support.

Good background reading for such a liturgical celebration would be Dobbels, *An Epistle of Comfort*; and Flynn, *AIDS: A Catholic Call for Compassion*.

*   *   *

Your study group may do as others have done and examine the church's stance regarding homosexuality. If you want to undertake such a project, a very useful resource is *Christians and Homosexuality*, available from The Other Side, 300 W. Apsley, Philadelphia, PA 19144. A good resource for hightening awareness of the mechanisms at work in prejudice in general is Cole, *Filtering People*. You may also consider asking representatives of the group Parents and Friends of Lesbians and Gays to address your group, if this organization exists in your community.

Resources for Further Study

Cole, Jim. *Filtering People*. Philadelphia: New Society, 1990.

Dobbels, William J. *An Epistle of Comfort: Scriptural Meditations and Passages for Persons Suffering from AIDS*. Kansas City: Sheed & Ward, 1990.

Flynn, Eileen. *AIDS, A Catholic Call for Compassion*. Kansas City: Sheed & Ward, 1986.

The Other Side. *Christians and Homosexuality*. (A study guide; see above for address to order).

Chapter Seven

Marvin, A Man on Death Row

The Imaginative Journey

I did wrong. I know it.

But when I sit here and think about the past, I always come back to the same question. Is what we do wrong *all* our fault? I wonder why so many people are so sure that the one who commits a crime is the only one responsible. I've had lots of time to read lately, and some of the books I've read make me ask questions like these. We believe that the individual who commits a crime is solely responsible; does this mean that society is *not* responsible for the individual? Does society have nothing to do with shaping people?

My crime does have a story—my story. The story of the world I was born into and grew up in. We Atkinsons were one of those families that struggle hard just to scrape by, and it has been that way for generations, as long as we can remember. When the Depression hit, Daddy says, times were even harder than usual. He was lucky if he got a pair of shoes each year to wear to school. The shoes that Grandpa Atkinson could buy came from a mail-order catalogue, and they rarely fit. Daddy had to walk about six miles to school. That was not very easy with shoes that pinched and hurt. Lunch was sometimes just store-bought bread spread with lard or bacon fat.

It's hard to study when your stomach is empty.

As the old saying goes, when it rains, it pours. In the middle of the Depression, several years of drought hit. After years of almost no crops came a year or two of high winds, and they caused the farm to blow away before Mama and Daddy's eyes.

That was the last straw. Daddy decided to give up farming. He had always gone shares anyway, and that meant he never got out of debt to the landowner and his store. In all the years he farmed, he never made more than enough to scratch the surface of debt. So after the drought he sold out and headed West.

People talk about moving West like talking about the Hebrew children going out of Egypt to the promised land. For Daddy and Mama, it was like going from one kind of slavery to another. On the farm, they had almost belonged to the big man. They worked daylight to sundown and hardly fed themselves. When they did make a good crop, it belonged to the landlord because they were in debt to him.

But at least they had the self-respect that comes from hard work and making your own schedule.

In the West it was different. Mama and Daddy, Imagene, Bert, Randoll, and little Tom were just another carload of ignorant hillbillies tussling for scarce jobs. When they got out West they didn't know anybody, or what jobs to look for. All they really knew was farming. They settled in a city and rented half of a double house in a run-down neighborhood full of other farm folks from our area. Nobody trusted anybody. The family on the other side of the house was loud and trashy. The husband drank and knocked his wife around. Daddy and Mama say some nights they never slept a wink, with the racket. I was born in that house.

One night as we slept, somebody broke in. Trying to rob us was like trying to get blood out of a turnip, but Daddy had some money tied in an old sock to buy shoes for the older kids come fall. Seemed like the thief knew exactly where to go. While Daddy watched from the bed, he went to the drawer and rummaged through it. He took that sock and a few other little things that Daddy had stored away in the drawer. Daddy saw the whole thing, but pretended to be asleep. He knew that if he tried to fight the thief, he might end up with a knife in his chest.

After that Mama just seemed to lose spirit. Her health had always been poor. One of the things that hurt her the most when they left the farm was leaving the graves of her two little ones that had died of fever. I was the baby of the family, and it was hard to watch her run down. Years of babies and never a moment's rest had made her look like an old woman, years older than she really was. Mama took to her bed and stopped trying to care for any of the family. Imagene was twelve, and she took over for Mama.

We Atkinsons had always kept together and made it the best way we could. I would say we were even a happy family, sometimes. Nights, we'd read to each other and sing songs. But Imagene tells me that this happened a lot more back home than out here.

Daddy tried to get some government help. The woman that came from the welfare office treated us like dirt. She asked questions about who slept where and how often we bathed and told us we didn't try to be clean. She hinted she might have to break up the family. So Daddy gave up on the government.

That's when I started stealing. In tenth grade, I had managed to get a part-time job in a canning factory. The evenings when I'd sit down with my books at the kitchen table, I was so tired, I'd go to sleep. Trying to keep up and make some money to help us out made me so mad that I started acting up at school. The principal kicked me out.

I made some new friends who laughed at me for working so hard, when I could get what I needed just by helping myself to it. They taught me the ropes. At first I just picked up this and that from stores. When I found out how easy that was, I decided to go big time.

My buddy Doody had a little pistol. One night we took it and held up a liquor store. We just pointed the gun and told the clerk to give us everything in the till. It was like taking candy from a baby.

Not long after this Mama passed away. I moved out. From stealing, I went on to drinking and drugs. Mama had never allowed a drop of whiskey in the house. She thought the bottle was the devil's own invention. I liked the thrill whiskey gave me. It made me forget I was a nobody, an ignorant hick. It made me forget that Mama and Daddy had worn themselves out working and had nothing to show for it. It made me stop thinking about the government lady and the school. When I drank, I could shut up the voice inside me that told me I was doing wrong.

I guess you can see where this story is going. One of the stores we robbed was bound to have a gun. One night we hit a little grocery store out in the sticks. When the owner reached into his register, he came out with a pistol and fired it at Doody. He hit him but didn't kill him. I had my own pistol, and I let the guy have it. We hit the road. The next day I saw in the paper that the man had died. Two days later, the police caught us trying to get away with a car from a farm lot.

I didn't have any kind of record. But the judge decided to throw the book at me. He said he wanted to use this case to show scum like me that no one can murder a man in this state and get away with it. The lawyer the state assigned to me didn't lift a finger to help me. Who cares what happens to nobodies like me?

What I can't stop thinking about is how different things *could* have been. *Should* have been. How different if anyone had seemed to care. Hard work and high moral standards don't seem to have gotten my family *anything*, except struggle and heartache.

It's not supposed to be this way in America.

Scriptural Reflections

The Word of God

[*Then the righteous will answer him*], "*And when was it that we saw you sick or in prison and visited you?" And the king will answer them, "Truly I tell you, just as did it to one of the least of these who are members of my family, you did it to me*" (Matthew 25:39-40).

Prayer Response

Lord, we forget to look for you in prison. We assume that those who end up there belong there. We excuse our indifference by passing judgment.

Remind us that people do not live and die unto themselves. We are all joined together in the social fabric of our neighborhoods and towns and cities and nations.

If any are in prison, we have all failed. We have failed to provide decent jobs, to educate, to help families stay together. Help us to ask if we imprison to hide from our own eyes the evidence of our callousness. Give us new eyes to see the humanity of all those behind prison bars. Give us eyes to see that you are in prison with them.

The Word of God

He unrolled the scroll and found the place where it was written: "The Spirit of the Lord is upon me, because he has anointed me to bring good news to the poor. He has sent me to proclaim release to the captives and recovery of sight to the blind, to let the oppressed go free, to proclaim the year of the Lord's favor" (Luke 4:17-18).

Prayer Response

Lord, you began your ministry by proclaiming that the jubilee year had come. The jubilee was release for prisoners and freedom for broken victims. You yourself ended your life as a prisoner unjustly accused and executed by the state.

Forgive us that we have domesticated your troubling message and example. Forgive us that we rest easy when our states put to death human beings made in your image. Forgive us that we are not outraged at the injustices and biases of our legal system. We commit ourselves to overturning these injustices and exposing these biases. We commit ourselves to creating a just society in which violence and theft will be less prevalent, because people's basic needs will be met.

The Word of God

O give thanks to the Lord, for he is good;
for his steadfast love endures forever.
Let the redeemed of the Lord say so,
those he redeemed from trouble
and gathered in from the lands,
from the east and from the west,
from the north and from the south.

Some sat in darkness and in gloom,
prisoners in misery and in irons,
for they had rebelled against the words of God,

> and spurned the counsel of the Most High.
> Their hearts were bowed down with hard labor;
> they fell down, with no one to help,
> Then they cried to the Lord in their trouble,
> and he saved them from their distress;
> he brought them out of darkness and gloom,
> and broke their bonds asunder.
> Let them thank the Lord for his steadfast love,
> for his wonderful works to humankind.
> For he shatters the doors of bronze,
> and cuts in two the bars of iron (Psalm 107:1-3, 10-16).

Prayer Response

Lord, your people praise you for your wondrous deeds of mercy. We praise you for your saving power. We give you thanks for your immeasurable compassion for us in our weakness.

And above all we give you glory because you are our Liberator, the one who overthrows all bondage and oppression.

The Word of God

Two others also, who were criminals, were led away to be put to death with him. When they came to the place that is called The Skull, they crucified Jesus there with the criminals, one on his right and one on his left. Then Jesus said, "Father, forgive them; for they do not know what they are doing." . . . One of the criminals who were hanged there kept deriding him and saying, "Are you not the Messiah? Save yourself and us!" But the other rebuked him, saying, "Do you not fear God, since you are under the same sentence of condemnation? And we indeed have been condemned justly, for we are getting what we deserve for our deeds, but this man has done nothing wrong." Then he said, "Jesus, remember me when you come into your kingdom." He replied, "Truly I tell you, today you will be with me in Paradise" (Luke 23:32-34, 39-43).

Prayer Response

To be your disciple is to accept your challenge to remember. We break bread in memory of you; in our worship and in the proclamation of your word, we remember you, we meditate on the significance of your life and shape our lives according to yours. We hand on the memory of you to gather together the church, generation upon generation.

To remember your death is to remember that you died in solidarity with criminals, that you offered salvation to the thief crucified with you. Even to the end, you reached out to the outcast, demonstrating that God's love does not recognize the cruel social boundaries we human beings erect. Give us hearts of compassion so that we may walk in the path you have trod before us.

Prayers from the Religions of the World

Walter Rauschenbusch

O God, we men and women in prison make our prayer to thee. We too claim thee as the Father [and Mother] of our spirit and the great Friend of our better self.

Men [and women] have passed judgment on us by our outward acts, but thou alone knowest all things. Thou knowest how some of us were burdened by the sins of our ancestors; and some were tainted with vice in our youth before we understood; and some made a brave fight, but the powers of evil were strong; and some thought they were doing right when they broke the law. We would hide nothing from thee, O thou Searcher of Hearts, but we pray thee to pardon the frailties and mistakes of the past, and in the years still left to us do thou build up our lives to noble manhood and womanhood. . . .

May all the great world of men [and women] be filled more and more with thy saving love, so that fewer men and women be snared in temptation, and those who go wrong may be turned back to the right without the need of prisons. Grant that our own experience may in some way help others, that so our life may not be lived in vain, but may add a little to the common good and joy of mankind in the better days to come.[39]

*　　　　　*　　　　　*

---

39. *Prayers of Social Awakenings,* 77-78.

Pope St. Clement of Rome

We beg you, Lord, to help and defend us. Deliver the oppressed, pity the insignificant, raise the fallen, show yourself to the needy, heal the sick, bring back those of your people who have gone astray, feed the hungry, lift up the weak, take off the prisoners' chains. May every nation come to know that you alone are God, that Jesus Christ is your Child, that we are your people, the sheep that you pasture.[40]

*   *   *

Grant peace and eternal rest to all the departed, but especially to the millions known and unknown who died as prisoners in many lands, victims of the hatred and cruelty of man [and woman]. May the example of their suffering and courage draw us closer to thee through thine own agony and passion, and thus strengthen us in our desire to serve thee in the sick, the unwanted and the dying wherever we may find them. Give us the grace so to spend ourselves for those who are still alive, that we may prove most truly that we have not forgotten those who died.[41]

*   *   *

Bishop Dehqani-Tafti of Iran

A Father's Prayer Upon The Murder Of His Son

We remember not only our son but also his murderers;

Not only because they killed him in the prime of his youth and made our hearts bleed and our tears flow,

Not because with this savage act they have brought further disgrace on the name of our country among the civilized nations of the world;

---

40. *Oxford Book of Prayer*, 74.
41. Mary Craig, *Blessings* (London: Hodder & Stoughton, 1979), 96.

But because through their crime we now follow thy footsteps more closely in the way of sacrifice.

The terrible fire of this calamity burns up all selfishness and possessiveness in us;

Its flame reveals the depth of depravity and meannness and suspicion, the dimension of hatred and the measure of sinfulness in human nature.

It makes obvious as never before our need to trust in God's love as shown in the cross of Jesus and his resurrection;

Love which makes us free from hate towards our persecutors;

Love which brings patience, forbearance, courage, loyalty, humility, generosity, greatness of heart;

Love which more than ever deepens our trust in God's final victory and his eternal designs for the Church and for the world;

Love which teaches us how to prepare ourselves to face our own day of death.

O God

Our son's blood has multiplied the fruit of the Spirit in the soil of our souls;

So when his murderers stand before thee on the day of judgement

Remember the fruit of the Spirit by which they have enriched our lives.

And forgive.[42]

---

42. Ibid., 135-6.

Actions on Behalf of Justice for the Imprisoned

In a number of journals that explore the socio-political implications of the gospel, prisoners advertise for pen-pals. You may wish to accept the invitation to correspond with an imprisoned person.

Among the journals that have such advertisements are *Sojourners*, Box 29272, Washington, DC 20078-5290; and *The Other Side*, 300 W. Apsley St., Philadelphia, PA 19144.

*   *   *

Some churches and parishes have organized prayer vigils and demonstrations against capital punishment. You may decide to sponsor such a vigil and demonstration. If you do so, you probably need to seek the advice of those who minister to prisoners and work to eradicate capital punishment. You would also need to consult your pastor.

*   *   *

The United States is among the few industrial nations who practice capital punishment (other such countries are the Soviet Union and South Africa). Statistics indicate that capital punishment does not deter crime and that the death sentence operates as a kind of lottery that favors white, educated, well-to-do people and penalizes minorites, the uneducated, or poor Americans.

Activists urge us to press our elected representatives to advocate abolition of the death penalty. You can write your congresspersons about this. Publicize what you learn regarding your representatives' views about capital punishment.

*   *   *

Churchgoers concerned about the death penalty have found it useful to organize study groups to examine capital punishment from a Christian standpoint. You may decide to form such a group. If you do so, pay attention to statistics showing that the death penalty is not a deterrent to violent crime, and that use of the penalty is heavily skewed against racial minorities and the poor. A good resource for such a study is Redekop, *A Life for a Life?*

*   *   *

Some other countries have proven that the penal system can contribute positively to the life of the nation by rehabilitating criminals. You may begin a personal study project to look at the philosophy and policies of such nations. Are there indications that the United States could do much more in the direction of humane treatment and rehabilitative programs? A good beginning resource for this project is Zehr, *Changing Lenses.*

*   *   *

Those who have studied the penal system are concerned about the tendency of the system to create more hardened criminals. They point out that juvenile offenders, some of whom have committed minor first-time offenses, are housed with older seasoned criminals.

These activists encourage us to scrutinize the penal system of our local community or state. Does your community place juvenile offenders in confinement with veteran offenders? Are serious efforts made to rehabilitate juvenile offenders and to assure that they will not become repeat offenders?

If you choose to follow this line of inquiry, a good starting point might be to contact a university professor who teaches sociology or criminology in your area.

*   *   *

Schools throughout the country have organized drug-awareness weeks. If your schools do not have such a program, help to get one underway; if one exists, take part in it. Try to ascertain the extent of drug problems (including alcohol abuse) among area youth, and plan programs to overcome the problem.

*   *   *

There is a recognizable link between juvenile unemployment and juvenile crime. Those ministering to prisoners note that if we want to make inroads into crime, one good place to begin is to see that adequate jobs are provided for youth. If you share this concern, you may wish to ask if something can be done to assure greater employment of teenagers—particularly youths from under-privileged and minority backgrounds—in your community. If you participate in a project to do this, you may urge the local associations of business people to address the problem.

Resources for Further Study

Redekop, Vernon W. *A Life for A Life?: The Death Penalty on Trial.* Scottdale, PA: Herald, 1989.

Zehr, Howard. J. *Changing Lenses: A New Focus for Crime and Justice.* Scottdale, PA: Herald, 1989.